NEW PARIS STYLE

PARIS STYLE

Danielle Miller

Photographs by
Richard Powers

363 illustrations, 342 in color

Thames & Hudson

CONTENTS

8

There's no shortage of style in the City of Light,

and its innate chic is reflected in the homes of its residents.

Parisians have long been held to be cultivators of flair

and sheer good taste, and the houses, apartments and

city crashpads of the taste-makers and creatives

featured within these pages do not disappoint.

Le bon chic is alive and well in the world's fashion capital.

In keeping with their global reputation, the French – and particularly the Parisians – continue to wield their enormous influence in the style stakes. But change is afoot, thanks to a new surge of fresh talent – from designers of haute-couture fashion to contemporary artists and specialist artisans – who are taking the reins of some of the city's time-honoured métiers. A new and burgeoning design scene is thriving, despite today's sensitive marketplace. Restaurateurs, perfumers and interior designers are also raising the bar. Whether it's the scenery that inspires such innovative vision and ingenuity, or the collage of skyward monuments and palatial museums, the timeless elegance of a bourgeois quartier or the edgy urban character that lies within a medieval enclave, the capital looms large in the design sensibilities of its residents.

It is easy to become seduced by other people's homes. A classic, Haussmann-era flat with sky-high ceilings and spare designer furnishings, or a modest, light-filled city pad decorated with a hint of make-do inventiveness and retro charm, can lead to lingering in front of estate agents' windows and dreams of calling in the removal men. The homes in this book evoke those familiar feelings of longing because they are so well considered, and so well executed; whatever style of interiors their owners have chosen to create, they have done so with genuine conviction. The homeowners are creatives in the fields of fine art, fashion, interior design and photography, among others, and have opened their doors to these most alluring, intensely personal of spaces. They share the philosophies that served as the starting point, and the fulfilment that comes from creating a space that is an expression of how they want to live. In some cases, it is a combination that draws on heritage and the knowledge and skill of local craftsmen, as design duo Elisa and Michael Catoir (p. 188) do at their two-bedroom apartment in the 15th, while other residences, such as the loft conversion of interior designer Pierre Yovanovitch (p. 100), balance fluid forms and natural materials within a masculine framework of heavy oak beams and angularity to result in a case study in rustic chic.

Style-wise, diversity is key, and there is no single look or unifying theme. The enfant terrible of the design world, Ora-Ïto (p. 50), for example, has filled his heritage-listed flat in the lively Marais neighbourhood with his own ultra-futuristic furniture and lighting designs, some of which have already reached icon status, along with heirlooms and antiques that include an antique suit of Samurai armour. The entire assemblage is a reflection of Ïto's fixation with shape and colour, and his belief that 'good taste is all about mixing it up and finding what works between old and new'. Even though his home is not a true representation of his work, he says, 'I really enjoy testing things out here. You could say that this is my style lab.'

In the heart of the Latin Quarter is the home of Michelin-star chef Thierry Marx and his partner, food photographer Mathilde de l'Écotais (p. 86), in which the exuberantly designed kitchen, as befits their career choices, is the focus. From its black-painted walls to cabinetry covered with Mathilde's molecular photography, it is clear that the couple

are not afraid of unleashing their design credentials on the heart of the home. Personal passions are also behind the design concept of the home of interior designer Florence Baudoux (p. 196). At her pièce de résistance near the Place du Trocadéro in the 16th arrondissement, Florence's intuitive eye for colour has created a glamorous setting in shades of grey.

The heady mix of Parisian form and style leads us on a journey that takes us around the spiral of arrondissements – from the historic 1st, in which are found the homes of actors (Marc Lavoine; p. 24), architects (Isabelle Stanislas; p. 30) and textile scions (Vincent Frey; p. 14), to lesser-known neighbourhoods such as Gambetta in the northeast 20th. It is in this culturally diverse neighbourhood that we find the area's latest urban tribe, the *bourgeois-bohèmes*, or *bobos*, a hip, laptop-toting crowd of creative twenty- and thirty-somethings. Sharing their patch of Paris are Hélène and Laurent Chapuis (p. 210), founder of a web-design company and a marketing whiz, respectively, who built a clean-lined, contemporary four-storey house, complete with a roof garden topped by a giant canopy sail, which incorporates the latest in eco-friendly design.

For those with the ingrained instincts of a collector and a love of amassing artefacts and objets trouvés, it is clear that someone like Jean-Christophe Aumas (p. 134), director of creative agency Voici-Voilà, has turned his ability to see beauty where others might fail into an art form, as is evident in his one-bedroom refuge, located on the vibrant western edge of the 10th arrondissement. The apartment's

design embodies the unscripted look of flea-market treasures and street finds, set against bold works of art and blocks of colour to form striking mises en scène, which makes the overall effect so compelling – you never know quite what to expect.

It is this unexpected quality that makes the homes of these Parisian style-makers so fascinating. This, together with the strong personalities of the homeowners that shine through each design, is what catches our eye and fires our imagination.

In the heart of tourist Paris, the wide boulevards and neoclassical façades of Baron Haussmann's vision are everywhere in evidence

On a plaque in the pavement in front of Notre Dame, on the Île de la Cité, 'Point Zero' marks the spot. Point Zero, or Kilometre Zero, is the point from which distances are traditionally measured – here in Paris, all roads lead not to Rome, but from the iconic twelfth-century cathedral. In fact, the origins of the city are much earlier, around 250 BC, when the Iron Age tribe, the Parisii, are known to have lived on the island. Two thousand years later the emperor Napoleon III, who saw Paris as a 'new Rome', set engineer and town planner Baron Georges-Eugène Haussmann the behemoth task of modernizing the city and imposing order on the jumble of medieval streets. Between 1853 and 1870, 60 per cent of Paris was rebuilt under Haussmann's guidance, with the aim of creating the unified urban landscape that is synonymous with the city today.

The first four arrondissements, all on the Right Bank, are clustered together at Paris's geographical centre. The 1st is a mix of upscale apartments and tourist outlets, along with such historic landmarks as the Musée du Louvre, the Jardin des Tuileries and the Palais-Royal, under whose arches can be found some of the city's most elegant boutiques. Nearby

are über-retail destination Colette, in Rue Saint-Honoré, and the Hôtel Ritz, in the Place Vendôme, where Coco Chanel famously lived for almost thirty years. Just to the north lies the 2nd, the city's smallest arrondissement at just under one square kilometre, and home to many of Paris's neoclassical temples to commerce. The former home of the Paris stock exchange, the Palais de la Bourse, designed by Alexandre-Théodore Brongniart and completed in 1825, is here, as are the old buildings of the Bibliothèque Nationale on the Rue de Richelieu (the bulk of the collections were moved to new premises in 1996).

One of the few districts that emerged almost unscathed by Haussmann's *grand projet* was the Marais, the original Jewish quarter, whose winding alleyways snake across parts of the 3rd and 4th arrondissements. It is home to a number of architectural gems, including the oldest planned square in Paris, the Place des Vosges, built by Henri IV between 1605 and 1612, and where Victor Hugo resided in the 1830s. The 3rd is the quieter half, home to the Musée de l'Histoire de France and a small but growing Chinese population, while the livelier 4th boasts the art mecca that is the Pompidou Centre, along with Notre Dame cathedral, on the Île de la Cité.

The transformation of the city continued up until the turn of the twentieth century, when Paris emerged as a vivid, sophisticated, richly cultural hub. Its appeal has hardly diminished in the century or so since – people may live in other countries, and travel the world over, but they'll always have Paris.

Bianca Lee Vasquez + Vincent Frey

At this former warehouse in the 1st, industrial chic is given a modern makeover with sumptuous fabrics and historic textile designs

There are some homes that capture our imagination, and stay in our minds forever. For Vincent Frey, it was not a house but a warehouse space within a centuries-old building that captivated him from the moment he saw it as a child. The warehouse belonged to his grandfather Pierre Frey, founder of the eponymous textiles company, and held 'thousands of metres' of beautiful fabric inside its walls. Two decades on, and it appears that Vincent, now CEO of the firm, also inherited Pierre's determination and innovative thinking. This newly reinvented home, with its strong linear, almost minimal outline, is now the perfect foil for the exquisite assortment of fabrics and furniture assembled by Vincent and his partner, fashion stylist Bianca Lee Vasquez.

The interior design of the house is seductive in its sophisticated comfort, accessorized with the couple's pick of textiles from the cavernous Pierre Frey archives (around 7,000 designs). The Braquenié-designed toile de jouy that flows from the double-height windows to such theatrical effect was the starting point for the whole scheme. The prelude, however, was more complex. 'The architects couldn't see how the design would work as we envisaged it,' says Vincent, explaining the task of re-engineering two individual spaces over two levels, accessed by communal stairs. Without electricity or plumbing, the city's rigid building codes only added to the problems. Eventually it was an old school friend, architect Marika Dru, who interpreted the simple brief to create a modern space that 'would not be unfaithful' to its history. In that spirit, the split-level home leaves visitors feeling as though they have entered into a contemporary haven, blessed with light, which is linked to the past. Over time, the flooring was pieced together like patchwork; rough-hewn concrete inlaid with glass brick brings a textural element to the dining area, along with pockets of the original *parquet de Versailles* – the marriage between industrial and antique has been consciously and carefully guarded.

'We've gone for warmth and plenty of texture,' says Cuban-born Bianca, who grew up in the Miami sunshine, which helps explain her love for the vivid colour used throughout the interior scheme. Having chosen a sofa in snappy tangerine-orange to set off the sitting room, Bianca recovered a pair of 1970s lounge chairs that belonged to Vincent's father, creative director of the firm, in sky blue, and propped large-scale photographic landscapes by Danish artists Nicolai Howalt and Trina Søndergaard against the wall. A graphic black-and-white rug anchors the space. The use of monochrome also sets the tone in the semi-open kitchen, a Valcucine design with a central island that features a section of the famed *Mur pour la paix*, or 'wall for peace', a reproduction (again by Pierre Frey) of artist Clara Halter's glass installation, inscribed with the word 'peace' in thirty-two languages, which stands at the foot of the Eiffel Tower.

Perched above the living space is the main bedroom, framed in calming shades of pale blue and silver. It connects to an alcove off the baby's room, named the *jardinette* by the couple for the botanical drawings that cover the walls. 'It made sense to bring some of this heritage into the home,' says Vincent. 'It feels right to us.'

Signature prints such as the 'Oberkampf' toile de jouy by Braquenié, chosen for the curtains, feature among several designs produced by the Pierre Frey textiles company.

In the sitting room, plexiglass chairs by Jacques Charpentier and Eero Saarinen's 'Tulip' chairs sit around a table formed from a piece of square-cut glass perched on top of stacks of magazines. On the floor is an 'Ovales' rug from Pierre Frey.

A dining table by Julie Prisca for Pierre Frey is paired with René Herbst's Bauhaus-inspired chairs from 1928 (opposite). Above, a pair of 'Opala' pendant lights by Hans J. Wegner illuminate a marble sculpture by Victoria Wilmotte (p. 154).

The monochrome theme continues into the glass and aluminium kitchen (above and left). The laminated wooden bar cantilevers to create an informal eating area in front of a fabric reproduction of Clara Halter's *Mur pour la paix*.

The redesign of this former textiles warehouse allowed for expansive openings on the upper level, particularly in the master bedroom, which give views over the dining area to the courtyard below.

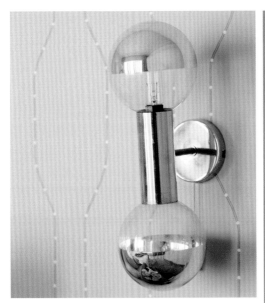

The couple's bed is flanked by vintage Staff Leuchten wall lights and Italian bedside tables from the 1970s. On the wall hangs *Alone With Others* by photographer Joakim Eneroth; the curtain fabric is 'Circus' by Jim Thompson.

A roll-top bath adds an old-fashioned feel to this otherwise sleek and minimal bathroom. Cabinets and plumbing are hidden within a dividing wall that separates the space from the master bedroom.

In the first-floor study (left), 'Sphere' pendant lights by Raak provide light through the new stairwell to the kitchen below. A 'Lady' armchair by Marco Zanuso from the 1950s sits on top of Braquenié's pop-coloured 'Art Deco' carpet.

A botanical print from Pierre Frey's extensive archives creates the verdant feel of the *jardinette* (right), a narrow alcove at the top of the stairs that connects to the nursery. The cardboard 'Angle' chair is by designer Julian Mayor.

Sarah+Marc Lavoine

High above the Rue de
Rivoli, a classic Haussmann
design has been reimagined
as a comfortable family
home with geometric
blocks of bold colour

Sarah Lavoine is, as well as an interior designer, a brilliant orchestrator, as her home attests. Outside the mirror-lined window of her study, decorated in shades of deep turquoise and black, are views of the Louvre and the Jardin des Tuileries, through whose linden trees can be glimpsed silvery flashes of the Seine. 'It's like being on a film set,' Sarah says of the location's cinematic quality – the reason behind her idea to line the window recesses with mirror, thus adding depth and making the most of both the views and the light.

The apartment, which she shares with her husband, actor-singer Marc Lavoine, and their three children – Yasmine, Roman and Milo – is a grand, four-bedroom affair, perched above the Rue de Rivoli in a Haussmann-designed building. It is decorated with a daring colour palette throughout to lend warmth and vigour to the ensemble of rooms, with their high, moulded ceilings, marble fireplaces and oak parquet floors. 'I'm not into uniformity,' says Sarah. 'I wanted to loosen it up, to deconstruct it. With colour you can do that; it adds dimension.' She speaks from experience, having recently launched her own range of paints for the home, like the *jaune-tournesol* (sunflower-yellow) used in the dining room, offset by geometric bands of black and white. Graphic works of art, black-and-white photographs and other standout pieces, such as the floor light by her friend Florence Lopez (see p. 92), add a further dimension. 'Colour gives a room a life of its own,' Sarah says. 'You learn that objects and art can have a strong impact on your space, and represent who you and your family are.'

Before launching her business, Sarah worked alongside her mother, interior designer Sabine Marchal, followed by a stint with decorator François Schmidt. Since then, she has hosted her own television series on interior style and designed a collection for French homewares giant La Redoute, along with interiors for the boutique hotel Jardin de Neuilly, located in the Parisian suburb of Neuilly-sur-Seine. Sarah has also opened a boutique one block away from her home, near Rue Saint-Honoré, where her designs, everything from initialled votive candles to sofas (mirrors of the one in grey linen in the study, and the pair in ecru in the sitting room), are sold.

The sitting room is a large and comfortable space that has been given the monochromatic treatment – in keeping with Sarah's view that 'where you have colour, you also need a room to pause'. Arranging the furniture centrally adds to the feeling of openness in the room. A canvas by French artist Fabrice Hyber dominates one wall, while an oversized panda sculpture by Chinese artist Jiji adds some fun to a corner niche beside the mantelpiece, itself home to a collection of tea-light holders designed by Sarah. There are tables in bronze by French designer Hubert Le Gall, and a lamp by Sarah's friend, design guru Philippe Starck, from the 'Guns' series for Flos, which sits atop Yves Klein's 'Table Bleue', an iconic design from 1963. In the entrance hall are displayed, collage-style, dozens of framed photographs and Polaroids from Marc's prized collection.

'There's a fine balance between sophistication and simplicity, which is very much the Parisian style,' says Sarah – a balance that she has achieved in a family home that is as fascinating to look at as it is comfortable and luxurious to live in.

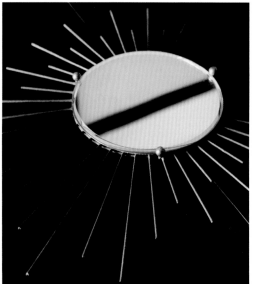

In the dining room, strong geometric patterning in yellow,
black and white creates a bold look, complemented by a
floor lamp designed by friend Florence Lopez.

26

Sarah herself designed the benches that sit alongside a custom-made dining table by Kara Mobilier (left). Artworks by Nobuyoshi Araki and Joseph Szabo hang on the walls, and mirror-lined window alcoves maximize the light.

The sitting room (below) is an open, inviting space, with a comfortable white linen sofa designed by Sarah, a pair of wicker armchairs by Charlotte Perriand and a bronze side table, in the shape of flower stems, by Hubert Le Gall.

In the bedroom, a Jean Prouvé-designed daybed sits beneath a painting by Ara Starck, daughter of designer Philippe (above, right), while a photograph by Alex Prager hangs above the bed (above). The Berber rugs are from Marrakech.

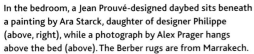

Isabella Stanislas

This architect's home near the Louvre is testament to her love for fashion and unerring eye for creating dramatic, modern interiors

The words 'be contemporary' are boldly emblazoned across an artwork in architect Isabelle Stanislas's bedroom – it is a maxim that she clearly adheres to. In the course of transforming her eighteenth-century apartment, which sits high above the arched arcades of the Rue de Rivoli, into a modern family home, Isabelle has given it an edge that is understated yet gracefully confident. 'It is a fantastic space, right in the middle of an area we all love,' she says.

Isabelle's apartment formerly served as the offices of Café Marly, located across the road, in the Louvre. Today, she shares it with her husband and their four young children. Complete with immense gilt mirrors, ornate mouldings, fireplaces and parquet floors sanded back to the grain, the historic space provides the canvas for Isabelle's decorative intermingling of past and present. These inherited period features are offset by key design pieces, from organically formed chunks of driftwood discovered on a trip to Bali, to low-slung benches and a piece from the 1960s, called 'Yeti', which is draped with yak fur and could be mistaken for a lounging bear. But the greatest surprise has to be the custom-made coffee table. Designed by Isabelle and Sabine Pigalle for fashion house Céline, it stands between a pair of deep sofas by Christian Liaigre and forms the centrepiece of the sitting room. The table lights up, featuring a daring, blown-up image of a flame-haired model. 'Fashion is a big influence', Isabelle says, 'as well as a bit of an obsession.'

As one half of the architectural duo So-An, meaning 'concept and composition' in Japanese, Isabelle and business partner Leiko Oshima can reel off an A to Z of clients as they complete one fashion-driven project after another, including minimalist boutiques and grand, baroque ateliers for the likes of Anne Valérie Hash, Sandro and Zadig & Voltaire. As far as the remodel for Isabelle's own home was concerned, the intent was to reconfigure the space into five bedrooms and, as she wanted to keep a large, open living area, introduce mezzanines to make the most of the double-height ceilings. In the master bedroom and bathroom, storage is completely hidden away and a dressing room fills the upper reaches of the mezzanine. Practicality is at the forefront, and is reflected in Isabelle's fluid designs, including the cushioned seating integrated into the luxurious, marble-lined bathroom.

'I kept things as simple as possible, because I wanted the home to be versatile enough for the kids to be able to go everywhere,' Isabelle says. 'But at the same time, I didn't want to vary the materials or the colour palette too much – I think that's key to finding the calmness of a space.' In keeping with this philosophy, the kitchen is simple, sleek and functional, with a solid, wooden bar extending from a row of cooking units in stainless steel. Industrial-style Nicolle Society stools and 'Conque' wall lights by Ronan and Erwan Bouroullec add to the contemporary feel, as do artworks by Ben and Philippe Pasqua and photographs by Edgar Martins and Peter Klasen. In the hallway leading from the kitchen to the children's zone, Isabelle hung four crisp, white shirts in a row, illuminated like an art installation. As she says, 'I wanted to add something fun and a little out of the ordinary to light the way.'

Innovative designs, like this coffee table created by Isabelle for Céline, define the contemporary space. In the hallway, a row of white shirts forms a different kind of light fitting.

At one end of the vast living space stands a backgammon table in leather marquetry by Deuce, paired with chairs by Harry Bertoia (above). In the kitchen (opposite), the worktop has been extended with a piece of timber from Bali.

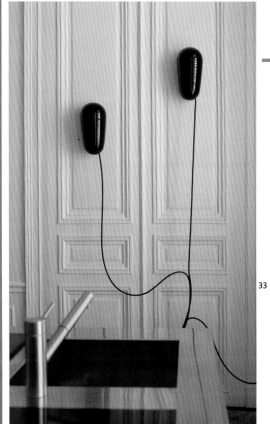

34

Functional elements are integrated into the bedroom design, including storage hidden within the headboard and seating to either side of the fireplace. The *Be Contemporary* print above the bed is by South African artist Kendell Geers.

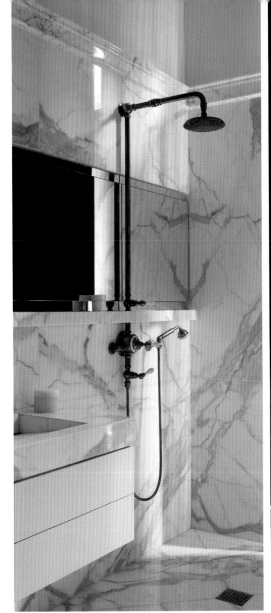

The clean, seamless design extends into the bathroom, entirely lined in marble, from the bath to the shelves. Isabelle designed the deep-cushioned seating, which lends a touch of softness to the all-out glamour of the room.

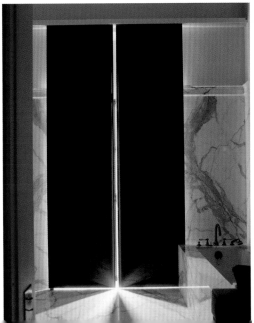

1

Joséphine+Emmanuel Gintzburger

An interior designer has transformed a neglected historic gem by introducing a little contemporary luxury to its rustic charms

The first thing visitors notice when walking into Joséphine and Emmanuel Gintzburger's seventeenth-century home are the striking works of art that cover the walls and line the floors, from a provocative image by the Chinese artist Jiang Zhi to works by the likes of Thomas Struth and Wilmar Koenig, whose homage to the baroque style takes pride of place above the mantelpiece. 'It depicts the most elaborate church you will find in the whole of Bavaria, in the centre of Munich,' says Joséphine. 'It is the only piece I have with me that relates to my hometown.'

The apartment illustrates Joséphine's love for art, fashion and design, honed by twenty years spent working for Louis Vuitton, Céline and Christian Dior, where she was head international buyer before leaving to start her own interior design business. She now runs her company from a glass-fronted atelier, located in the lively Montorgueil markets enclave and set within a cobbled courtyard overlooked by her split-level apartment. Before its transformation by Joséphine and Emmanuel, worldwide retail director at Yves Saint Laurent, the flat was in a derelict state. 'Everything needed to be retouched in some way,' she says. Partitioning walls were removed to create

a more organized layout and larger, brighter spaces, which now house the kitchen, a TV room and the bedroom of the eldest of their three children. The upper level, with its loft-like feel, contains further bedrooms.

Joséphine was keen to restore the original features, and to incorporate elements that would suit a busy family life. Where the original floors could not be saved, she used poured concrete instead, a functional choice that serves as a counterpoint to the home's antiquity. In the main living space, a palatial setting with rustic beams and soaring windows, Joséphine painted the floors a blue-grey colour, and set off a pair of low-slung sofas by German furniture company Rolf Benz with a surgical floor light with a retro feel. The extra-long, lacquered coffee table was designed by Joséphine herself; in the corner is an antique African bust, discovered while on a trip to Kenya. Throughout the flat is a sense of fun, evident in the funky, floral vintage lamps and 'Rose' chair in hot-pink velvet by Masanori Umeda for Edra.

In the romantic master bedroom, gold and turquoise walls are complemented by crisp, white paintwork, a lilac-coloured bed by Ligne Roset and a pair of antique wall sconces that provide flickering, atmospheric candlelight. Large-scale photographs by Cindy Sherman and Li Wei hang on the walls, and in the corner stands a mannequin covered in silk jacquard, which doubles as repository for the vintage

brooches collected by Joséphine with her mother, alongside a classic 'Arco' floor lamp designed by Achille Castiglioni for Flos. Retro and contemporary influences continue in the bespoke kitchen, designed by Joséphine, with a hot-pink and red colourway that serves as an effective contrast to the industrial-chic backdrop of steel and concrete. Once again works of art, here by Judith Huemer and Andy Warhol, are the focus. A chandelier that belonged to her grandmother adds to the playful sense of kitsch. After all, says Joséphine, 'a home should be full of the kind of contrasts that create an impact and draw on emotions' – an effect that she achieves.

Masanori Umeda's 'Rose' chair is paired with a framed drawing by Italian sculptor Guiliano Vangi. On the floor is an antique alligator skin, a memento from Cape Town.

Sofas in grey velvet from Rolf Benz and a pair of black-lacquer coffee tables designed by Joséphine lend a modern edge. The 'very kitsch' floral table lamps and surgical-style floor lights are from local antiques dealer Alexis Lahellec.

Against rustic wooden columns are sconces discovered at the Renoncourt antiques shop in Saint-Germain-des-Prés. An artwork by Wilmar Koenig, hanging above the fireplace, is flanked by hand-blown lamps from Pairpoint Glass.

In the kitchen, the industrial look is softened by accents in pink and red (opposite). The angular red wall light by Arteluce and the Arne Jacobsen-designed chairs were discovered at the Clignancourt flea markets.

In the master bathroom, originally the kitchen, concrete surfaces are given a softer edge through the incorporation of mirrors and a chandelier that dates back to the 1800s. An artwork by Alexander Timtschenko hangs above the bath.

Wallpaper from the 'Royale' series by Designers Guild, together with worn stone floors, give the bedroom a romantic feel. A 'Snowdonia' bed by Éric Jourdan for Ligne Roset is the focal point; above is *Falls to the Earth* by Li Wei.

Hervé Sauvage

One of the city's most feted set designers has created his own mise en scène in the 2nd – one that pays homage to the art of the Surrealists

It takes a few seconds for one's eyes to adjust when moving through the visual labyrinth that is Hervé Sauvage's apartment. A stuffed lamb stands atop a pedestal table of mossy rocaille, and Grecian busts, other forms of taxidermy, and austere-looking dolls and glass domes are all displayed with a stylist's skill in the three reception rooms leading from the entrance hall. But this eccentric, slightly surreal approach to interior decoration is only what one would expect from one of Paris's best-known set designers, who has worked his magic by creating unconventional designs for the likes of Hermès, Bulgari and Tom Ford.

From the classic Thonet bistro chairs that date back to the 1930s, to the Charlotte Perriand-designed daybeds (which Hervé bought 'a long time ago when it was still possible to find them around the flea markets'), everywhere is evidence of a collector with an appreciation for design. 'The Surrealists had a big impact on me as a teenager,' he says, 'and a part of

that still seems to find its way into most things I do.' Originally from the village of Picardie, in northern France, Hervé studied art history at Nanterre before being snapped up by Nina Ricci to produce window installations and sets for the fashion house's runway shows. Hervé says that he had never heard of set designing 'until someone said I should give it a try', noting that 'set designer' doesn't translate into French. Hervé's first photographic shoot for French *Vogue*, with the late fashion director Isabella Blow, led to a commission to design the sets for Nicolas Ghesquière's first collections for Balenciaga.

In his work, Hervé is hands-on with every detail. To bring his atmospheric sets to life, he has help from the same builder who put together Hervé's inventive shelving design at home, painted in deep coral, which

covers each of the non-working fireplaces. In the second sitting room, Hervé inverted the books so that instead of multicoloured spines, all that is visible are rows of textured ivory – a visual trick that he once used on a set. The latest addition to the room is a sculptural installation in the form of a workbench, complete with mirrored tools, which was a gift from an artist friend, Jean-Christophe Vaillant. It shares the space with mid-century armchairs, reupholstered in black-and-white fabric by Charles Eames for Kvadrat, which sit in front of the window overlooking the busy boulevard de Sébastopol, and edgy photographs by the artists Jean-Charles Blais and Vibeke Tandberg. In the bedroom, a patchwork throw by Babeth Rambault picks up on the rich shades of the shelving and the soft, grey tones of the painted doors and boiserie. The original parquet floor, worn smooth with age, has been stripped bare and bleached.

For his set designs, Hervé is drawn to the more obscure objects and antiques that he has tracked down on his habitual visits to the city's flea markets. Naturally some of these have found a place in his own home, such as the collections of vintage chairs, ceramics and glassware. But is there a limit? 'I could sell everything tomorrow and start again, apart from my daybeds,' he says. 'I try not to hold on to everything, even if I'm tempted by the things I've made myself. I have to be rational.' After two years of designing, decorating and adding to his apartment, Hervé concedes, 'I think I've hit the maximum.'

Curios and objets d'art fill every inch of this designer's light-filled space. Among the more unusual pieces is a workbench with mirrored tools (opposite), the gift of an artist friend.

A favourite piece is a daybed designed by Charlotte Perriand (above), one of a pair. Just visible to the side is a stuffed lamb that Hervé used for a shoot for a *Wallpaper* magazine story, entitled 'Les fables de la Fontaine'.

In the custom-designed bookshelves, books are arranged back-to-front, a decorator's trick Hervé first used on a commercial set (opposite). The wooden stools are another star find from the Clignancourt flea markets.

49

The black-painted dresser (above, left) that Hervé describes as his *petit cabinet de curiosités* is a family heirloom from the early nineteenth century. In front of it is a Thonet-designed mirror-top table and chairs from the 1930s.

A corner in the bedroom provides a quiet spot for working (opposite). Pulled up to the desk is a 'Magis' chair by Konstantin Grcic; the armchair next to it is a rare design by Swedish furniture designer and architect Bruno Matheson.

III Ora-Ïto

This mover and shaker of
the design world makes
his home in a spectacular,
heritage-listed apartment,
set in the centre of the
lively Marais neighbourhood

Designer Ora-Ïto, born as Ïto Morabito and now
known by the name of his brand, is recognized for his
distinctive, futuristic designs, which embody a sense
of aerodynamic vitality. His split-level apartment
in the buzzing Marais district is full of them; think
2001: A Space Odyssey and old-world, new-world
contrasts being played out against the backdrop of a
listed building. In the sitting room, a cobalt-blue and
white polyurethane sofa and accompanying chairs
from Ïto's Ora-Gami range for Steiner, composed
in geometric planes and curves, share space with
armchairs designed by Ïto for Frighetto and an
'ecological bookcase' for French furniture company
Artelano, all of which incorporate his trademark
combination of curved and flat surfaces.

'I'm not into uniformity,' Ïto says, describing
the rich blend of fluid-form antiques, heirlooms and
modern art. 'Good taste comes from knowing how
to mix pieces from different eras in a way that is
interesting and elegant.' This might sound a little
counterintuitive coming from a man at the cutting
edge of product design, but, in keeping with this
philosophy, the most unpredictable of objects sit
alongside the ultra-modern forms that underpin

the design scheme. An antique suit of Samurai
armour, for instance, keeps watch over Richard
Hutten's vibrant red 'Sexy Relaxy' chair from 2002
and an Edo-period (1615–1868) Japanese panorama.
Overhead is a mobile in luminous acid-yellow,
designed by an artist friend, Xavier Veilhan.

Marseilles-native Ïto's father is luxury-goods
designer Pascal Morabito, and his uncle was Yves
Bayard, one of the architects behind the Musée d'art
moderne et d'art contemporain in Nice, so it is not
surprising that his earliest influences were aesthetic
ones. At the age of nineteen, after dropping out of
design school, Ïto masterminded a set of iconoclastic
virtual products in 3D and labelled them with
luxury-brand logos, including Louis Vuitton's
'LV's and Nike's swooshes. Instead of lawsuits,
commissions ensued, and Ïto now counts Citroën,
Bic, Lee Cooper and aircraft maintenance firm
Sabena Technics among his clients. Having founded
the Ora-Ïto studio in 2002, Ïto's seemingly endless
product range belies his thirty-five years, and in 2011
he was named Chevalier des Arts et des Lettres, one
of France's highest honours.

Back in his apartment, on the walls hang
artworks by Louis-Marie de Castelbajac and French
art collective Kolkoz, while a larger-than-life-size
portrait of Michael Jackson, swathed in gold, is by
the spiral staircase. Up the stairs is the glamorous
mezzanine, now painted black to contrast with the
jewel-like colours of the original decorated beams
that first attracted Ïto to the apartment. 'It's like
walking into another century,' he says. 'I have the
history of France right there on the ceiling.'

In the bedroom is another of his prototype
designs, this time in the form of a Formula 1-inspired
bed. 'I need to live with my pieces, giving them a
test drive, so I'm constantly shifting things around,'
Ïto says. 'I like the fact that the place is never static
and keeps on evolving. But on the whole, it doesn't
actually reflect my work. For me, this is something
more of a style lab.'

The planes and curves of Ïto's 'ecological bookcase', designed
for Artelano, are a nod to the design aesthetic of the 1970s,
the decade in which the artist was born.

53

At the base of the ultra-modern spiral staircase, leading up to the black-painted mezzanine, are chairs from Ïto's Ora-Gami range for Steiner (opposite, bottom). The acid-yellow mobile (above) was designed by artist Xavier Veilhan.

54

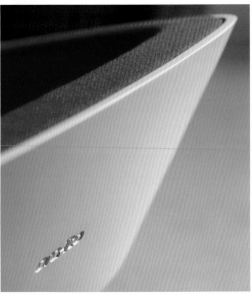

In the main living space, a Japanese suit of armour and
modern, sharp-edged furniture add to the highly individual
decorative scheme (opposite). In the bedroom (above),
a Formula 1-inspired bed incorporates integrated storage.

Corrado de Biase

Opulently decorated in gold, black and bronze, this luxuriously reinvigorated pied-à-terre in the 3rd oozes cinematic glamour.

Entering designer Corrado de Biase's apartment is a bit like walking into the pages of the *Arabian Nights*. Palm trees and shimmering shades of gold lend an exotic, glamorous feel to the place, while soft furnishings, such as the wine-coloured divan in the living area, are embellished with metallic embroidery. Unusual objets d'art – from taxidermy to brass lamps – crowd every available surface.

Corrado, a native of Puglia, in southern Italy, began his career designing shoes for Fendi in Rome, followed by stints at Yves Saint Laurent and John Galliano, and now shows his own haute-couture collections on the Paris runways. Now that he is based in the city, Corrado was very specific in the look that he wanted to achieve for his one-bedroom pied-à-terre. Although he cites Pierre Cardin, Courrèges and the Memphis group among his fashion influences, when it came to his flat, he was, he says, inspired by a scene from *Mulholland Drive* (2001), David Lynch's steamy film noir: 'When the lead girl walks into that amazingly lit interior and there is a warm glow all around her, that is what I wanted to recreate – that similar 1970s feel of warmth – by way of layering rich and reflective surfaces.'

As with his clothes and shoe designs, there is much in the detail. Take the wall treatments, for example: the glossy black tiles that line the kitchen walls are the same as those used for the Paris Métro stations, while the palm trees that bedeck the walls of the living space, which Corrado confesses to 'obsessing over' in the quest for the perfect metallic finish, have the added benefit of introducing yet more gold to an already rich scheme, and providing a textural background to the open-plan layout. Clearly inspired by the louche look of the 1970s, Corrado has scoured the flea markets and antiques shops of the world for finds. The wall sconces that hang in the bedroom – from an Italian film set that he happened across in Clignancourt market – and the multicoloured ceramics from Vallauris, near Antibes,

along with mirrors and lamps from Rome, all date from the decade. They are displayed against such key furniture designs as a dining table by Jean Prouvé, surrounded by red leather chairs (also from the 1970s), and figurative drawings by Corrado himself, which give the home a particularly personal touch.

For the bathroom, Corrado called upon the talents of a set designer friend in Milan, who sourced just the right fittings in, of course, gold. 'There was no way I was going to do a premeditated total look,' Corrado says. Instead, he chose to follow his own design guides: 'The contrasts help to soften the light at night, and the courtyard. Having space to breathe outside means everything to me, coming from my part of the world. It's what I grew up with.' Southern Italian influences continue with the delicate curtains, hand-embroidered by Corrado's mother and grandmother, which filter the light and introduce a little old-world charm to the resolutely exotic surroundings.

In short, this luxurious, exotic haven is a world away from the Parisian hustle and bustle below. Although the flea markets and vintage shops of the city have become his hunting ground of choice, Corrado's unique design vision reached far beyond the confines of the catwalks to create an internationally inspired, richly decorated retreat.

The palm trees and liberal use of gold throughout this fashion designer's apartment lend the space an exotic feel reminiscent of something out of the *Arabian Nights*.

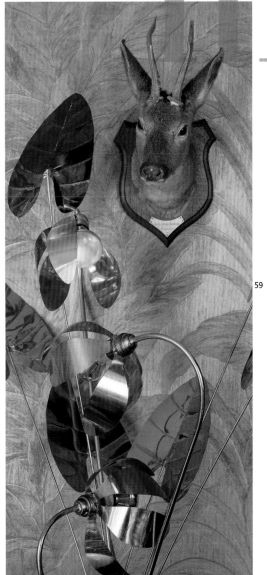

Rich, reflective surfaces help to maximize space in this petite duplex, and provide a striking backdrop to the collection of unusual, mostly vintage pieces dotted throughout the apartment.

The Jean Prouvé-designed dining table and surrounding chairs are flea-market finds, as are the white ceramic vases, which date from the 1940s and were discovered at Spitalfields Market in London.

The high-gloss black surfaces of the upstairs bathroom are accessorized with gold fixtures, sourced by a set-designer friend, which give the space a high-luxe Italian feel in keeping with Corrado's Puglian heritage.

Armel Soyer + Gilles Pernet

No longer a diamond in the rough, this polished workshop-turned-family home in the Haut Marais retains hints of its utilitarian past

As a little girl, gallerist Armel Soyer would visit an old jewelry workshop that belonged to her stepmother's grandmother, who ran the business, and watch the intricate pieces being coated in fine layers of gold before being packed off to the fashion houses, including Sonia Rykiel and Yves Saint Laurent. Surprisingly, she says, it wasn't the jewelry

itself, but rather the atelier and its 'rough charm' that left such a lasting impression – so much so that fifteen years later, Armel, then a savvy twenty-five-year-old, bought the premises and fulfilled her childhood dream. Fast-forward a decade and the place she described as a 'diamond in the rough' is now a polished jewel, tucked away down a shadowy passageway and surrounded by the contemporary art galleries and edgy design 'happenings' that have put the neighbourhood on the art-world map.

Today, hidden behind an opaque, glass-panelled façade is a thoroughly modern family home. Armel was intent on keeping the industrial spirit of the space – from the rugged stone floor that extends along the entrance way to the exposed wooden and steel beams – but the interior layout was dramatically altered to open out in a series of fluid living spaces devised by her close friend, architect Céline Carbonell. Since moving in, Armel married photographer Gilles Pernet, whom she had met in her previous career heading communications for Lalique, and started a family. With the arrival of their two young sons, Armel says the house has proved to be the 'completely child-friendly' home she hoped that it would become.

The living space is entirely open plan, with a relaxed vibe that comes from the family's mix of practical vintage furnishings, most of which have been picked up at various flea markets around the city. At the foot of the stairs, a Goyard trunk doubles

as a holdall for shoes, while a pair of school desks, sourced from the flea markets of Clignancourt, stand in a corner of the dedicated play area. With charcoal-coloured resin underfoot and a few works of contemporary art on view, there are also photographs on the walls from Gilles's *New York* series, which can be viewed at the couple's shared gallery and photographic studio, just steps away from the home.

An olive-coloured chaise longue from the late nineteenth century forms a divide between the living and dining areas, where the kitchen, tucked into a corner niche, is hidden away behind a sliding screen. Armel designed the dining table, topped in exotic Macassar ebony and set on industrial cast-iron legs. Around it are Italian rattan chairs from the 1950s and leather chairs by Jens Risom (who designed the first chair for Knoll in 1941). The latter were a 'super-rare find', discovered by the couple at a roadside *brocante* en route to their country house in Normandy, where there is 'plenty of space to keep all the old things we can't resist buying'.

There are more contemporary examples, too. Perched on the ebony ledge by the window is a lamp in the form of a delicate golden birdcage, designed by Pierre Gonalons (voted *Wallpaper* magazine's 'best breakthrough designer'). Upstairs in the bedroom, a pair of marble side tables are topped by Eiffel Tower lamps, also by Gonalons, who is set to exhibit, along with other young designers, at Armel's new gallery.

The 'Falcon' chair by Sigurd Ressel (opposite) is from the nearby Galerie Alexis Lahellec; on the ledge sits a Lalique vase from 1931. The ceiling lights are by Céline Carbonell.

The house's industrial origins are reflected in the furnishings, including the dining table, which was designed by Armel. Above a pair of vintage school desks in the play area hangs an artwork from Gilles's *New York* series (left).

66

The bedside lamp and marble side table (left) are both
by Pierre Gonalons, one of the designers represented by
Armel's nearby gallery. Beyond the bed is a colourful niche
that forms the children's bedroom (above).

A wall cabinet designed by Céline Carbonell (above) in the children's area doubles up as a desk. The orange wicker chair is a flea-market find. In the bathroom (right), shimmering mother-of-pearl mosaics add a touch of glamour.

IV

Valérie Mazerat

A humble canal boat, moored in the shadow of the Place de la Bastille, has been stripped down to essentials and softened with earthy colours and textures

The idea of living on a boat can seem idyllic, conjuring up the impression of a carefree, bohemian existence. Yet on the canalside edge of the Place de la Bastille, smart, efficient design and panoramic views of the city's iconic architecture also feature heavily. Aboard her reinvented Dutch barge, which originally dates from the early 1900s, architect Valérie Mazerat says: 'It's another world, which takes you far away from any ordinary semblance of the everyday.' The slower, gentler pace of living on the water suits Valérie and her young daughter, Margot. 'There is a sense of freedom that you don't get living ashore, and time definitely slows down,' she says.

Valérie has spent the past two years, 'on and off', instilling a new state of domestic comfort into the barge. Not that the idea of being afloat is something new for this canal habitué; for over a decade, Valérie has been running her architectural practice, together with two colleagues, from another boat moored a short stroll and a footbridge traverse over the same canal. Recent projects include interior designs for the chic fashion and interiors shop Merci, located in the Haut Marais, and Bonpoint, the French childrenswear boutique with outposts around the world.

The boat had already had a long working life along the Dutch waterways until a previous owner converted it into a liveable space. 'He took an old train carriage from the 1920s and plonked it on top of the boat,' Valérie says. By the time she came across it, the entire structure needed gutting – the floors, walls and ceiling of the main living space (essentially the carriage addition) were all rebuilt through to the bow, which now contains two cabins and a bathroom. A new wood-burning stove was installed, while the galley kitchen and the dining and coffee tables were all custom-made in steel, a material deliberately used by Valérie 'to preserve the mood and industrial feel', in recognition of the boat's robust past.

The quest, she says, was about creating a comfortable domestic vibe that was easy to live in, as much as maximizing storage in the tightest pockets of space – it is impossible to squeeze in a wardrobe that stands at 2m high. 'Now everything reminds you of what you consume — water, energy. It makes you think twice about most things,' Valérie adds, 'but it's in my nature to keep things simple. You just can't be frivolous' – an observation that sums up the thinking behind the decor. Once the restructuring process was out of the way and painting and decorating could begin, 'in beautiful shades of grey', the decorative philosophy began to evolve. It is clear that Valérie likes to keep things simple and real, and the warm, textural materials around the boat have been kept

to an earthy palette, from the natural linen fabrics from Merci and Caravane and hand-woven rugs to industrial Jieldé lamps, and even the worn leather 'butterfly' chair brought back from Morocco.

Valérie's approach to restoring and decorating her home is very hands-on, and she has been known to wear denim overalls at the weekend. 'You can't be afraid of getting your hands dirty,' she says, 'there's always something that needs fixing. But there is a real community-minded energy along the canal, and we are surrounded by a friendly bunch of neighbours.' Out on deck, Valérie and Margot like to sit under the canopy, even sleeping there in the summer months. At night, the lights of the Bastille illuminate the sky. 'It's a beautiful way of life. I would say it's the city's best-kept secret.'

The cabin has been completely transformed from its former function as a train carriage to reflect the architect-owner's love of natural materials and simplicity in design.

Life is tranquil on the still waters of the Bassin de l'Arsenal, with views of the colonne de Juillet on the Place de la Bastille (right). On deck, a canopy allows some privacy when reclining on simple daybeds, covered in linen from Caravane.

The interior layout has been designed with practicality at the forefront. The dining table (left) is a custom-design in steel, and the vintage chairs are by Arne Jacobsen. The desk lamp is from a local second-hand shop.

Valérie Mazerat

A salvaged Christmas decoration from Merci sits in the window above custom-designed shelving (above). In the main cabin (right), fabric brought back from Morocco covers the seating on either side of a wood-burning stove.

72

Soft pink bedlinen and a sheepskin rug add warmth to
Margot's bedroom (above). In Valérie's cabin (right), a Danish
bureau from the 1950s, along with one of the Arne Jacobsen
chairs, sits beneath a portrait by photographer Serge Anton.

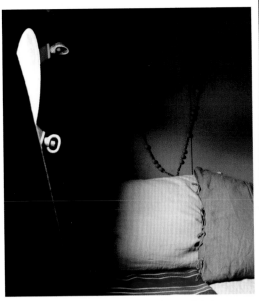

Shades of taupe and charcoal grey and natural timber surfaces unify the interior space, which has been designed with simple, day-to-day living in mind. Even the head (below) is an elegant, if functional, space.

The rich variety of Parisian society is here, from the cafés of the Latin Quarter and Saint-Germain to the red-light district of Pigalle

Stretching across the 5th and parts of 6th arrondissements, the Latin Quarter has been the centre of bohemian Paris for centuries. Named after the language spoken at the University of Paris when it was founded in the twelfth century (the university is known today as the Sorbonne), the quarter takes in the myriad streets that surround what was the Left Bank's student and intellectual hub, and continues to lure to its multitude of cafés and bistros those tourists and locals seeking a little of the spirit found in the books of Hemingway, Camus and Sartre.

Also in the 6th, Saint-Germain-des-Prés extends down to the Seine from the Jardin du Luxembourg – created for Henri IV's widow, Marie de Médicis – where the Musée du Luxembourg, built in 1750, is located, the first museum of its kind to be dedicated to the arts. As an only-in-Paris amalgam of art, fashion, politics and literature, the neighbourhood is where publishers, antiques dealers, fashionistas and actresses rub shoulders, and can also boast being the birthplace of jazz in France. Around the Église de Saint-Germain-des-Prés, the oldest abbey in the city, dating from AD 543, are the temples of Parisian café society – Les Deux Magots, Café de Flore, among

many others – which played host to numerous literary greats since the latter part of the nineteenth century, and later the entourages of Dalí, Chagall and Picasso, who lived and painted in nearby Rue des Grands-Augustins from 1936 to 1955. In 2000, the cobbled square in front of the church was renamed in honour of Jean-Paul Sartre and Simone de Beauvoir.

The neighbouring 7th arrondissement is one of the most elegant residential areas in the capital (past residents have included Yves Saint Laurent, Serge Gainsbourg and Jane Birkin), as it was in the 1800s when it first became home to various foreign embassies and National Assembly members. France's most recognizable architectural icon, the Eiffel Tower, is here, erected to commemorate the 100th anniversary of the French Revolution, and among the cultural institutions are the Musée d'Orsay, housed in the former Paris-à-Orléans train station, and Musée du Quai Branly, designed by Jean Nouvel, who also designed the Institut du Monde Arabe in the 5th.

Across the river, to the north of the textile quarter Sentier, lies the 9th, where crowds gravitate to the area's glass-domed department stores and the Palais Garnier, home of the Paris opera. The 9th's seedier end is home to the (mostly x-rated) Place Pigalle. In its heyday, the area's racy reputation attracted such artists as Manet and Toulouse-Lautrec, who captured the dancers of the Folies Bergère in their canvases. Between these two extremes lies the world's oldest auction house, Drouot, and an intimate residential quarter full of ornate, pre-Haussmann buildings, popular with *bobos* such as Stéphane Ghestem (p. 108) and Sacha Walckhoff (p. 116).

Jean-Philippe+ Sophie-Anne Delhomme

In the Latin Quarter, overlooking the Jardin du Luxembourg, a stylish, light-filled eyrie is home to a pair of globetrotting creatives

Illustrator Jean-Philippe Delhomme has many strings to his artistic bow. A chronicler of fashion, style, and what's new and happening in the worlds of art and design, his drawings are familiar to readers of *Architectural Digest* (France), *GQ* and the *LA Times*. He has produced award-winning ad campaigns for clients that include Visa, Barneys New York, SAAB, among others, as well as being a poet and author of novellas and illustrated satires such as *Design Addicts* (2007) and *The Cultivated Life* (2009). Thoroughly in touch with the modern scene, Jean-Philippe also blogs under the nom de plume, 'The Unknown Hipster'.

His wife Sophie-Anne, long-standing art director for the weekly newspaper *Courrier International,* is also an author; her novel *Quitter Dakar* (*Leaving Dakar*) describes her experiences of growing up in Senegal. The couple met when they were art students at the École nationale supérieure des Arts Décoratifs in Paris, and over the years have made the journey back and forth between New York, where Jean-Philippe maintains a studio near Union Square, and Paris, to which they recently returned with their teenage son after a year-long sabbatical across the pond. Their new home in the Latin Quarter is like a luminous eyrie, set high above the Boulevard Saint-Michel, overlooking the fabled Luxembourg gardens. 'Not many homes in the city have this sense of elevation,' says Jean-Philippe, 'where the scenery really becomes part of the interior.'

His workspace is located at one end of the long sitting room, where a small, teal-coloured guéridon by Konstantin Grcic for SPC, a recent gift from Sophie-Anne, stands in front of one of the bay windows. Here, Jean-Philippe can be found painting landscapes

in saturated colour of the park and a skyline studded with Paris's architectural icons, viewed as tourists rarely see them. He describes his output as 'realistic, minimal, spontaneous', which could also be said of the top-floor apartment. Transformed from a *chambre de bonne* (or maid's quarters) into a long, simply designed, open-plan space, the apartment boasts an opening in the ceiling that soars up towards a skylight, which provides all-day evenness of light.

The pair has pulled together an assortment of furniture and artworks, which are offset by the sleek, grey granite that frames a fireplace at one end of the space. 'We basically transferred over what we had in New York, which was mostly picked up at flea markets or garage sales,' explains Jean-Philippe. Among their finds is a 'special' armchair by Danish designer Ib Kofod-Larsen, dating from 1950 and discovered at the Hanson Place flea market in Brooklyn, along with a 'cheap' picnic-turned-dining table, patched and mended, the subject of a string of anecdotes, one of which involved a near-collision with a deer while it was strapped to the roof of the car. This room also features an orange 'Swan' chair by Arne Jacobsen and a white leather sofa from Ligne Roset, pointing to the pair's appreciative eye for the classics of modern design.

To gather material for his illustrations, Jean-Philippe has been known to make visits to Colette, Le Bon Marché and, in particular, art galleries to seek out unusual characters; as he says, 'I like to keep a tab on what's going on in design.' At home, the pair prefer to keep to a style that is 'simple and practical, with things like souvenirs that tell a story'.

Among the couple's favourite pieces is an original painting, hanging between the windows, by French illustrator Raymond Savignac for the poster *Garap*, dating to 1953.

Perched on the top floor of a late nineteenth-century building, this elongated loft space – a former *chambre de bonne* – combines Jean-Philippe's work studio and the family living area.

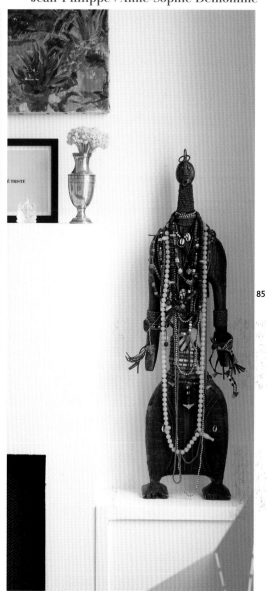

The simplicity of the architectural elements is enhanced by an informal approach to the decor. In the bedroom, an African figure is adorned with rosary beads collected by Sophie-Anne when she lived in Dakar (above, right).

Mathilde de l'Écotais+ Thierry Marx

A star chef and a food photographer go for all-out glamour in this edgily funky apartment in Saint-Germain-des-Prés

The new apartment of Thierry Marx, a well-known chef with two Michelin stars to his name, and his partner, food photographer Mathilde de l'Écotais, always promised to be different. Situated in the heart of the Latin Quarter, it is both their family home, and the focus of their working and creative lives. 'The kitchen is definitely the soul of the home', says Mathilde of Thierry's domain; her photographic studio is conveniently set up in the room next to it. Here, she produces the zoomed-in imagery that accompany the recipes Thierry creates for his cookbooks, which go by the names of *Daily Marx*, *Sweet Marx*, *Easy Marx*, and so on. It's a dynamic working partnership, one that spills over into the decor of their home.

The couple developed the layout of the kitchen to function as both a culinary workshop and a family-orientated space. 'We devised the detailing together,' explains Thierry, 'but I had more of a hand in the functionality, while the aesthetics were Mathilde's doing.' Turning the surfaces of the kitchen units into a canvas, Mathilde covered them with her own creations. She painted the walls in matte-black and decorated the kitchen table with another of her images, this time in the form of a giant

fish, finishing off the look with a Christian Cubina-designed chandelier. In contrast to the ultra-plain, utilitarian kitchens that have become the norm, this unusual version makes for a brilliantly dynamic space. Mathilde's food-inspired photography is also on display throughout the rest of their spacious four-bedroom home – the first the couple have shared together. 'Furniture-wise, we moved in with very little apart from Thierry's futon,' Mathilde remembers, 'so we almost had to start from scratch.'

The pair have since managed to fill the apartment with fun-loving flea-market finds, including a pinball machine and retro-style toy helicopter, both of which are favourites of Mathilde's daughters, Mahaut and Rosalie. Other adventurous items include a coffee table on oversized castor wheels with an aquarium on top, designed by Mathilde, which continues on the aquatic theme. Among her other designs are tripod stands that have been reincarnated as floor lamps, and glass domes filled with such unusual items as a collection of vintage light bulbs, while flanking the fireplace are her photographic takes on caviar. Contemporary pieces of furniture also have their place, including a dining table by Ferruccio Laviani, big enough for all the family to gather around and enjoy what must be the finest home-cooked meals in Paris.

Moving to the capital from Bordeaux, Thierry – considered one of the pioneers of modern

gastronomy in France – has taken up the helm at the five-star Mandarin Oriental Hotel, located in the Rue Saint-Honoré, on the Rive Droite, which makes for a scenic bicycle commute to and from work across the Seine. At home, Thierry continues to invent gourmet delights for his growing collection of cookbooks. The time he enjoys most is 'very early in the morning', when he is at peace in the kitchen – a place that has become 'a great space in which to reflect on ideas'.

Mathilde's zoomed-in, food-inspired photographs are found throughout this spacious flat, located near the Place Saint-Sulpice in the centre of Saint-Germain-des-Prés.

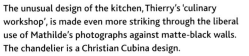

The unusual design of the kitchen, Thierry's 'culinary workshop', is made even more striking through the liberal use of Mathilde's photographs against matte-black walls. The chandelier is a Christian Cubina design.

90

The focal point of the sitting room is an oval coffee table, with a top fashioned from one of Mathilde's photographs. It features hundreds of tiny fish, echoing the live fish swimming in the glass bowl on top.

Glass domes filled with found objects and repurposed tripod stands add to the eclectic mix. Yet more of Mathilde's photographs, which feature in partner Thierry's cookbooks as well as in her own titles, adorn the walls.

Florence Lopez+
Patrick Hernandez

This rooftop atelier-turned-private gallery in Saint-Germain-des-Prés echoes the Parisian flair of its designer owner

The home of antiques dealer Florence Lopez is perched on the top of an eighteenth-century building in Saint-Germain-des-Prés, awash with soft daylight, thanks to its generous north-facing windows. Built in the 1920s, the former artist's atelier effectively doubles as an exhibition space, open to clients by appointment, which is entirely reinvented once or twice a year because, unusually, everything in the house is for sale. Florence is also an interior designer, and has turned her creative talents to designing interiors for a string of private homes around France.

Originally from Bordeaux, Florence returns there on weekends to join her architect husband Patrick Hernandez, but during the week, she lives in the two-bedroom atelier with their teenage son Raphaël. This is her creative space, where, aside from antiques dealing, she designs all manner of interesting things, including lamps for the home of Sarah Lavoine (p. 24), and a Herbert Bayer-inspired fresco, in shades of russet and blue, for her own dining area. This creative spirit, she says, is inherited. Her mother was a 'multitalented tour de force', designing theatre sets and haute-couture gowns that were sold in her boutique in Bordeaux, and Florence remembers the décor of her family home as constantly changing.

After studying art history in Bordeaux and Paris, Florence worked for the grande dame of interior decorators, Betty Sherrill, in New York, before returning to Paris, where she spent the following seven years working for decorator Jacques Garcia. The same day Florence quit his studio, she discovered the atelier by chance. 'I fell in love with it,' she says, 'It was so intimate and personal, even though it wouldn't equate to the size of a client's entrance hall!' Inside are all manner of exquisite objets d'art and pieces of furniture – some of which are museum-quality, others are deeply personal, mostly dating from the 1920s to the 1960s – which sit alongside a Harvey Probber-designed sofa, a coffee table by Giò Ponti and Angelo Lelii lamps, together with works by contemporary French designers Thomas Lemut and Bruno de Caumont. 'For me, all these things interact with one another like characters engaging in a dialogue,' explains Florence, 'and then there are particular pieces that will spark a story.'

Florence was inspired to paint one wall in the sitting room flamingo-pink in memory of the colour (long since faded) of her 1940s Dorothy Draper-style sofa, and as a tribute to the pioneering American decorator – one of her great influences. She has since recovered the same extra-long sofa in anthracite silk linen, and hung above it a delicate sculpture in white resin by Fabrice Langlade, alongside a painting, dating from 1947, in a 'blue prism' form by Argentinean artist Gyula Kosice. Shades of deeper blues and greys are used throughout the room, which is topped with a skylight that continues the pink and blue theme in a graphic, trompe-l'œil effect. In the bedroom, a tapestry by Michel Deverne, covered with 'Klein-esque blue' shapes, is used as a rug, while curtains made from vintage dress fabric frame the rooftop views and reflect the inlaid lithographs in a pair of commodes designed by Piero Fornasetti.

Florence displays her painterly talents as an homage to Herbert Bayer and the Bauhaus through a fresco in the dining area and an embellished skylight in the sitting room.

94

A painting by Alfred Reth above an Italian velvet sofa, Angelo Lelli lamps and a sculpture by István Beöthy are among much-loved pieces collected from around the globe, all of which add a touch of luxe to the space (opposite).

The colour scheme in Florence's home-cum-gallery changes almost as often as the furnishings come and go. Among the pieces on show is a blue-lacquered desk by Bruno de Caumont, which sits beneath the window (above and right).

Florence had this Michel Deverne tapestry, here used as a rug, in mind when painting the bedroom this particular shade of intense cobalt blue (opposite). In the corner is an Alvar Aalto armchair and commode by Piero Fornasetti.

VII Pierre Yovanovitch

At this loft conversion
in the 7th, quality materials
and a soothing palette
provide a masterclass in
minimalist chic

Pierre Yovanovitch, the owner of this elegant fourth-floor loft apartment in the smart 7th arrondissement, knows a thing or two about creating a look. He began his career designing men's prêt-à-porter collections for Pierre Cardin, and worked for the fashion legend for eight years before embarking on his new role as an interior designer. When speaking of his former employer, Pierre mentions Cardin's 'extraordinary creative energy, his eye for proportion and the textural qualities of fabrics'. Those qualities have filtered into Pierre's own designs, and are visible in the refined choice of fabrics used throughout the apartment, from cashmere and velvet to sheepskin and mohair, all in shades of white, ivory and sand.

Having grown up in Nice, Pierre set up his business in Paris soon after transforming his previous apartment – a duplex opposite the Elysée Palace – more than a decade ago. 'One thing led to another and I was asked to decorate flats for some friends,' he says. 'And then for friends of friends, and so it evolved.' He now leads a design team of twelve at his studio in the Place de la Madeleine, bringing his own chic and understated look to a discreet, high-style – 'not high-fashion' – clientele.

Pierre lives on the top floor of a former *hôtel particulier* that dates back to 1672, and which he describes as 'one of the most beautiful in the area'. Inside, a vast living space is dominated by vaulted ceilings and rustic oak beams, and light spills in through curtain-free, heavy-set dormer windows, which frame views of the treetops, mansard roofs and Juliet balconies. The space exudes an easy chic through the milky tones of the walls, the powder-grey woodwork and soft whites of the furniture, and is configured around a Hans J. Wegner desk and a spiral sculpture from the 1970s that Pierre discovered at an antiques shop in New York.

Other modern pieces include a coiling paper-tube screen by pioneering architect Shigeru Ban, a conversation piece of a sofa carved from dark-stained oak, and a travertine table, around which friends gather for dinner parties. Swedish and American designs from the 1920s through to the 1940s (Pierre's favourite local antiques dealer is Eric Philippe), a coffee table in cork by Paul T. Frankl, a cuddly armchair by Danish architect and designer Flemming Lassen and sculptural chairs by James Mont all provide curvy counterpoints to the rugged masculinity of the oak beams. A painting by the British artist Mark Francis hangs above the fireplace, one of Pierre's own designs.

The original structure of the apartment was in 'an ideal condition' when Pierre found it, and needed no interference other than the addition of a skylight to the central corridor. Beyond the sparse, functional kitchen and bathroom, classically styled in limestone, is a second bedroom, now turned into a gym. 'The place is really very private to me,' Pierre says. 'I intentionally planned the apartment without a guest room so I could have it to myself.'

Pierre's luxurious home is in a building that dates from the seventeenth century, which for many years housed the salon of the fashion designer and artist, Louis Féraud.

The design scheme is underpinned by a palette of neutral earth tones, set off by a collection of furniture-design classics. In front of a cream-coloured sofa sits a curvy coffee table in cork by Paul T. Frankl (opposite, top).

A vintage armchair by Flemming Lassen provides a cosy spot by the window (left). Beside a limestone fireplace designed by Pierre (opposite), a 'Diamond' chair sculpture by French artist Franck Scurti hangs in the corner.

The uncluttered design and restrained palette extend to the bedroom (opposite) and limestone bathroom (above). In the hallway (left), floorboards are left untreated to echo the rugged masculinity of the oak beams of the ceiling.

Stéphane Ghestem

In this architect's pre-Haussmann apartment in the 9th, sharp detailing and a bold use of colour define the overall look

When one's career is devoted to creating some of the most soigné interiors in the world's most elegant city, a laid-back personal refuge is a must. For architect Stéphane Ghestem, that escape, situated in the more subdued northeastern part of the 9th arrondissement, channels his distinctive style and combines the kind of slick and innovative detailing that gives this period two-bedroom space its edge.

Stéphane taught architecture for over a decade at L'École nationale supérieure d'architecture de Paris-La Villette before setting up his own practice, Abstrakt Architecture. He also consults on a variety of commercial projects in China and India, but still maintains that 'one needs to find the balance between being modern and historically aware', which he conveys seemingly without much effort (see Yvan Mispelaere; p. 140). For his own homes, Stéphane has redesigned, lived in and moved through several projects in the city and the South of France, where he is originally from. He lives in his present apartment with his partner, José Masso, an art dealer who focuses on the works of contemporary graphic artists at the stylish shop Saint Honoré Wallcoverings in the 1st arrondissement.

The apartment previously served as the surgery for a medical practice, and was 'split into tiny rooms that had been left untouched since the late nineteenth century, kitchen included', Stéphane explains. 'It was in a shabby state, but there were no surprises structurally, just the old wallpaper that had to be stripped back.' Each of the rooms, overlooking the trees in the central courtyard four storeys below, is flooded with sunlight – helped by the removal of some of the original partitioning walls. Finding quality materials and skilful artisans is akin to discovering the Holy Grail for any designer, and Stéphane and José have gone to great lengths to ensure that the original detailing in the ceiling mouldings and cornices, and the brass inlays surrounding the fire hearth, have been sympathetically recreated and carried through seamlessly throughout the new floor plan.

Dominating the sitting room are shelves designed by Stéphane in the form of a pod-like display case, with each pod filled with books arranged, colour-coded, to look like a graphic installation. The stucco panelling used throughout the space, also designed by Stéphane, contrasts with the original cornicing; integrated into the stucco are sculpted lights, formed to resemble wallpaper peeling away. A striking oak suite, dating from 1950 and designed by Guillerme et Chambron, was discovered by the pair at the famed antiques markets of L'Isle-sur-la-Sorgue in Provence,

and recovered in olive-coloured wool. The rug was dyed in contrasting deep tangerine; coffee tables, too, received the makeover treatment, and their original clear glass tops were replaced with black mirror.

In the bedroom, Stéphane's black 'diamond-point' cabinetry looks striking against shades of soft blue-grey. 'I like the idea of modifying an existing piece, rather than having to look for something different every time we move,' he says, having given the Giò Ponti dining chairs a lift with powder-blue paint. Above hangs a much-loved Venini chandelier from the 1930s, spotlighting the black-and-white 'Eclipse' series on the wall by artist Claude Closky.

Strong design elements sit against coolly minimalist interiors to create a well-ordered, elegant space in a quiet residential neighbourhood in the 9th.

A floor-to-ceiling bookcase lends a sharp, graphic edge to an otherwise elegant space, as does the minimal light fitting, shaped to look like peeling wallpaper. The hallway leads to the kitchen, a second bedroom and the bathroom.

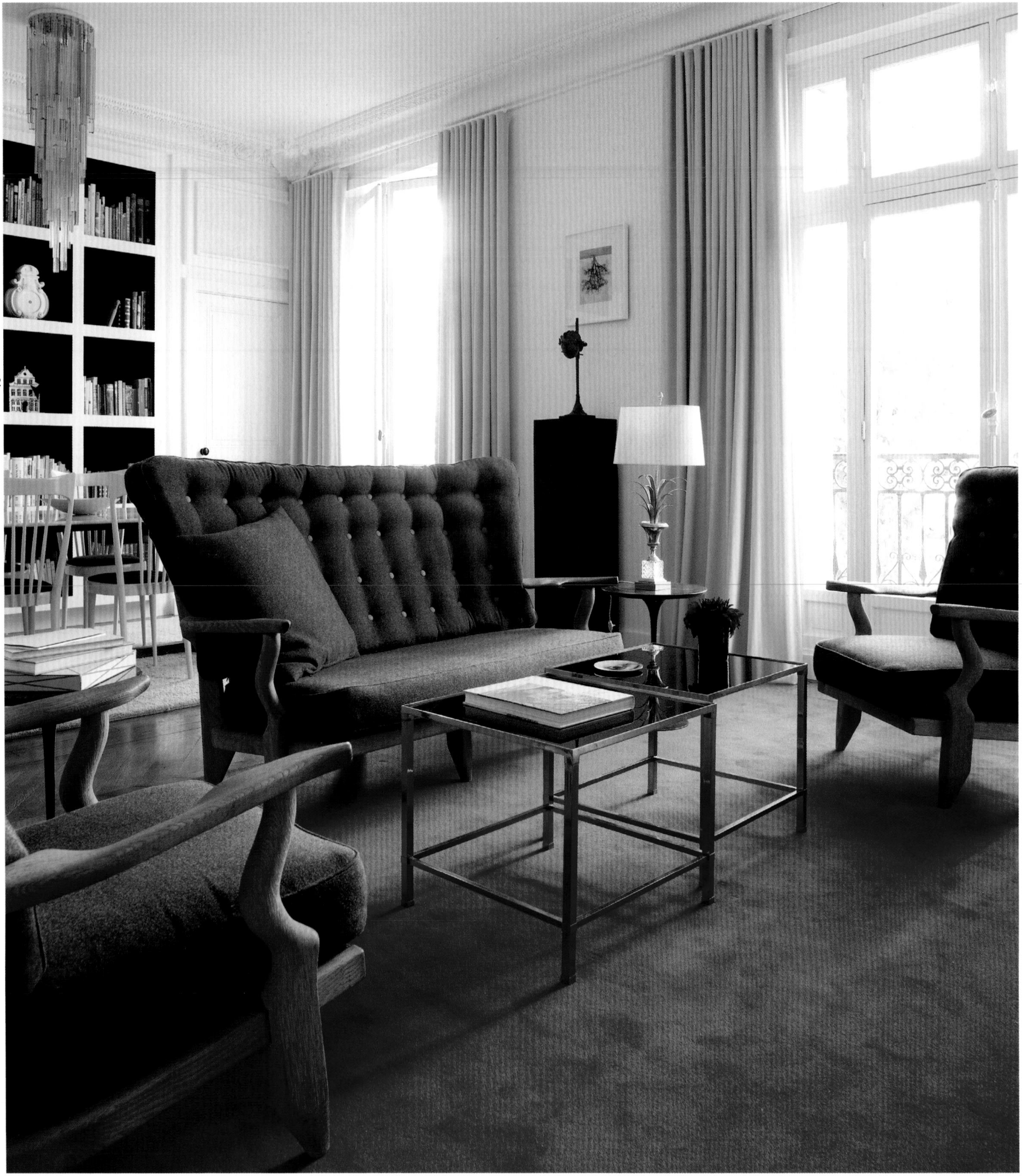

A custom-designed rug in tangerine injects bold colour into the sitting room. On top sits an oak suite by Guillerme et Chambron, recovered by the couple in olive-coloured wool, among other design classics.

114

The colour scheme of the master bedroom was dictated by the colours of the large abstract painting by Corsican artist Toussaint Mufraggi, which hangs above the bed. At the end of the hallway is a glimpse of the marble-lined bathroom.

The original glass-panelled doors of this former medical
practice maximize the daylight that flows into the hallway.
A vintage starburst mirror is propped up on the fireplace
next to a blue vase by Piero Fornasetti.

IX Sacha Walckhoff

Located on the Right Bank, the private refuge of Christian Lacroix's creative director is full of exuberant colour and delightful excess

'I am aware of my home looking a bit mad, even a little surreal, in a Cocteau-esque sort of way,' says fashion designer Sacha Walckhoff. 'But if you look at it like a collage, it really pieces together my story.' Sacha's story begins by the side of fashion designer Christian Lacroix, for whom he worked for a colourful seventeen years. In 2009, the economic downturn prompted Sacha to step into his mentor's shoes and take up the design helm of the company. 'It was a wonderful adventure,' Sacha says of those years with Lacroix. 'But now we are reshaping the house, and bringing it to a new generation with a focus on the brand heritage, in line with the essence of Lacroix: mix and match, pattern and print, old and new.'

In Sacha's two-bedroom, Charles X-era apartment that he shares with partner Pascal Ferrero, the master's influence is apparent. The space is filled with a riot of colour and a touch of visual chaos. Dominating the entrance hallway is a stuffed zebra,

seemingly leaping out of the wall, while an oversized fan by Dutch designer Maarten Baas (famous for his burnt furniture), vintage erotic art and a life-sized porte-torchère, draped in chunky African beads – souvenirs from early Lacroix days – add to the wildly imaginative space. The boldly coloured fabrics that cover furniture throughout the apartment are from Christian Lacroix Maison, the home textiles range Sacha has produced with Designers Guild. The black and white-striped sofa cushions echo the zebra hide underfoot, while another zebra-print rug, this time in the adjacent study, is also part of the range, as is a digitally printed toile on the wall depicting a nineteenth-century scene of Arles, the home for a time of Vincent van Gogh and the birthplace of Christian Lacroix. This is flanked by old army

camouflage nets, stretched across the window panes, which were found, like much else in the apartment, on one of Sacha's regular weekend treasure hunts around Paris's flea markets: Marché Malik, Porte de Vanves, Paul-Bert in Clignancourt.

'I could never limit myself to a single period or style,' Sacha says, attributing his eclectic tastes to his multicultural upbringing – his mother is French and father is African, he was raised in Lausanne and studied fashion in Barcelona. He prizes his mid-twentieth-century furnishings, such as the Charlotte Perriand-designed stools in the master bedroom, as highly as artworks by friends including Sophie Le Chat (p. 182) and ceramicists as diverse as Picasso and Marcel Wanders, whose colourful creations are propped up on shelving designed by Mathieu Matégot. There are hyper-surreal sculptures everywhere, and guests passing through the study on the way to the kitchen might be surprised by a life-sized statue of a man, by French artist Daniel Firman, who stands in a tangle of rubber inner tubes. 'I love works like these that show a fun side,' Sacha says. 'I couldn't live without them.'

A stuffed half-zebra seems to leap out of the wall, while a pair of 'Ptolomeo' bookcases by Bruno Rainaldi flank the entrance hallway that leads to the sitting room (opposite).

Collections of all sorts vie for space. Walls are filled with collages of framed drawings and pictures, and a life-sized porte-torchère is draped with beads from Africa and mementoes from the heady days at Christian Lacroix.

In front of the striped sofa, with its cover and cushions from Christian Lacroix Maison, is a Roger Capron-designed coffee table and a tweed-covered armchair by Pierre Paulin (below). In the corner is a 'Clay' fan by Maarten Baas.

The zebra-striped rug and jewel-bright fabrics that cover the armchair and spindle-legged stool are from Christian Lacroix Maison. In the hallway hangs a photograph by David LaChapelle, which features shoes designed by Sacha himself.

121

A sculpture from Daniel Firman's 'Bubble' series (above) stands in the study beside a 'Pleated Pleat' stool by Yael Mer and Shay Alkalay of Raw Edges. In front of the bookcase is a group of 'Moon Rock' floor lamps by André Cazenave (left).

Black-and-white bedlinen and a polka-dot carpet by Ege
add to the monochrome palette of the bedroom (above).
The kitchen's more utilitarian style is reflected in the
'c' chairs by Xavier Pauchard, a 1930s design (opposite).

IX

Éric Allart

An award-winning apartment block in the shadow of Sacré-Coeur is the home of this Renaissance man of the contemporary art scene

For Éric Allart, maintaining three different careers — as an art and antiques dealer, an interior designer, and the proprietor of a PR agency (which numbers Corrado de Biase among its clients; see p. 56) — has inevitably led to the creation of a small empire. Geographically, he has the city covered, from the PR showroom in the 1st arrondissement and a design gallery in the 7th, to a second home within the Marché Paul-Bert in Clignancourt in the 18th, which also functions as an exhibition space for twentieth-century design. In addition, Éric designed a home collection, featuring a circular, faux-Gothic mirror in polished steel, one of which now hangs above the mantelpiece at his primary residence.

This main home is situated down the hill from Montmartre, not far from Sacré-Coeur. It is on the fourth floor of an early twentieth-century apartment building, regarded by many as the most beautiful in the neighbourhood, which was the recipient of an architecture prize from the city of Paris in 1901. Inside, Éric has remodelled the space and reorganized the layout into a refined refuge. 'Most of the apartments in the building are huge,' he says, 'but I think I ended up with one of the smallest.' Throughout the space, earthy and neutral tones have been layered to create a warm atmosphere, with gentle eau de nil on the walls, outlined in *blanc cassé*, and floors stained in a deep walnut colour and topped with cowhide rugs. The addition of folding doors in the main living area allow it to be opened up into one large space, or subdivided into smaller, cosier rooms.

Among the pieces on show are those by creators that Éric likes to collect for himself, including Willy Rizzo, the Italian photographer-turned-designer whose portrait of Salvador Dalí graces the hallway and black-lacquered bookcases flank the fireplace. In front of the fireplace, a leather director's chair by Danish designer Børge Morgensen sits beside one of Éric's favourite pieces — a Fred Brouard-designed glass-topped coffee table, with an organically formed base in aluminium. Polished steel lamps in the form of a cross sit on either side of the sofa, a French design from the 1970s, while above hangs an artwork by his friend, Françoise Baudru. 'I started collecting paintings back in my teens,' Éric says. 'But at the age of eighteen I discovered antiques, focusing on items from the 1940s, '50s and '70s, in particular.'

Having worked with all kinds of homes around Paris, Éric has naturally picked up a number of design secrets. To bring daylight into the hallway, for example, he hung giant mirrors and designed their frames to match the casing around the doors for a seamless finish, while glass-panelled doors were fitted throughout to help the flow of natural light into such areas as the bedroom. In contrast to this opulent style, an entirely minimalist design in rich wenge wood was conceived for the bathroom. The kitchen moves off in yet another direction, as Éric wanted the 'feel of country house'. The original tiles of the chequerboard flooring were restored, on top of which sits a bluestone-topped dining table, designed by Éric himself, around which friends often gather for a meal. 'There's a wonderful ambience,' he says. 'They stay late and never want to leave!'

The faux-Gothic mirror above the fireplace is from Éric's own collection. On either side is a pair of Lucite lamps, designed by Philippe Jean, from the 1970s.

Éric designed the bluestone-topped table to complement the rustic feel of the kitchen, which incorporates the original exposed bricks and tiled floors. It sits beneath an Arts and Crafts ceiling light in silk and brass (opposite).

A Fred Brouard-designed coffee table from the 1970s provides a focal point in the sitting room (above), a warm space painted in eau de nil. In the hallway (left), a portrait of Salvador Dalí hangs above a pair of French garden chairs.

'A universal city where every step upon a bridge or a square recalls a great past, where a fragment of history is unrolled at the corner of every street.'

Goethe's description of Paris neatly encapsulates the charms of the cluster of arrondissements that curve around Paris's eastern end, from the 10th in the north, rubbing shoulders with Pigalle, down to the 13th on the Rive Gauche. The 10th, best known as the home of Paris's main train stations, the Gare du Nord, the terminus for the Eurostar, and the Gare de l'Est, from where the Orient Express first departed for Istanbul in 1893, also boasts the picturesque Canal Saint-Martin, a former working waterway that connects to the Seine via a serene, tree-lined passageway. The canal's appeal has only recently been rediscovered, and the surrounding semi-industrial area had been gentrified by creatives who saw the potential in its derelict buildings.

To the east is the 11th, home to the old working-class neighbourhoods of the *l'est populaire*, including Oberkampf, Faubourg Saint-Antoine and Bastille. When the Opéra Bastille opened on 14 July 1989, to commemorate the bicentennial of the storming of the fortress, it helped to attract a broader public to the arrondissement, which in turn set real-estate prices skyrocketing. For centuries the centre of furniture-making, the area borders Le Marais in the 3rd and 4th and the neighbourhoods of the 20th, Belleville and Ménilmontant, and runs from the Place de la Bastille all the way to the Place de la République.

In the 1990s, the 12th arrondissement received its own boost with the construction of the Promenade Plantée, the world's first elevated urban parkway, which runs along the abandoned Vincennes railway viaduct. Completed in 1993, the park extends almost 5km to the edge of the city, and its success spurred the development of the High Line in New York. In nearby Bercy, the regeneration of the old warehouses, which formerly stored wine that arrived on barges from Burgundy, sparked the creation of an entirely new, even fashionable, neighbourhood.

Tucked into the southeastern corner of the Left Bank, the 13th arrondissement encompasses the city's most contrasting landscape. Home to a vibrant Chinatown, and, much like the 12th, to many other large immigrant communities, the neighbourhood was previously a rustic outpost, where low rents are still a feature. Here are vast swathes of high-rise apartment blocks, with the picturesque hilltop village of La Buttes-aux-Cailles beyond. Once deemed the *faubourg souffrant* – the 'ailing suburb' – the arrondissement is now home to the new Bibliothèque Nationale, and the district's latest revival scheme, Paris Rive Gauche, and its centrepiece, the MK2 multiplex, designed by architect Jean-Michel Wilmotte, whose daughter Victoria (p. 154) now lives in the 11th.

Jean-Christophe Aumas

Flea-market finds and a vibrant, eclectic style turn conventional design on its head at this creative director's apartment in the 10th

Nothing is too fantastical for creative director Jean-Christophe Aumas, who has combined blocks of colour, vintage finds and bric-à-brac in a way that appears random and effortless. This is a look, however, that requires careful planning. 'Home is like my work,' he says. 'A series of things and objects that I love, which are put together in a way that feels right to me.' His one-bedroom apartment, from the corniced ceilings to the stripped-back parquet floors, is filled with originality and coloured with a vibrant palette, all of which, he explains, had a logical evolution. The acid-yellow painted across the dining-room wall picks up the colour of the table legs, and is repeated on the living-room wall. These subtle, unifying effects might go undetected by the untrained eye, but it is clear that this is just the kind of detail that Jean-Christophe thrives on.

Pink, yellow and Palm Springs: 'I love the retro glamour the combination conjures up,' he says, leaning back against his prized Arne Jacobsen sofa, a 1958 original and 'a lucky find' that he snapped up at the Saint-Ouen flea market. 'I used black and geometric details to contrast with it.' Throughout the apartment, an obvious passion for the pre-loved

is in evidence, from the chunky white ceramic screen by Eileen Gray, picked up in Antwerp, to the leather-top stools by Charlotte Perriand and a dining table from the 1950s, which began life in a Paris university. Among the building works carried out were raising a partitioning wall between the bedroom and the bathroom – a cool, dark space painted in teal – which in turn formed an alcove and ample space for a wardrobe. Doors were also removed to add 'some extra flow'.

Originally from Aix-en-Provence, Jean-Christophe came to the capital to study textile design at L'École supérieure des arts appliqués Duperré, and he soon turned his attentions to creating window displays for the likes of Lancôme and Christian Lacroix. After taking charge of Louis Vuitton's visual identity in the 1990s, just as the brand was undergoing a renaissance with Marc Jacobs at the helm, Jean-Christophe established his own design firm, Voici-Voilà, in 2005, where he numbers John Galliano, Chloé and Diptyque among his clients. Jean-Christophe's creative work has undoubtedly influenced his approach to his home, which was originally part of a former convent, built three hundred years ago on the slender Rue des Petites-Écuries, an area that is currently seeing an influx of a new media types. Recently, Jean-Christophe bought shopfront premises for his business in the same road, conveniently located a few doors away from his home.

The designer is no dilettante when it comes to sourcing unique treasures. 'For me,' Jean-Christophe says, 'it has to have a soul and an added something

that makes me fall for it.' His unerring instinct has led him to glossy vintage ceramics from Sicily, which now sit alongside tiny porcelain figures on the marble-tiled kitchen bar, designed by the man himself. Projects past and present are also in evidence in the form of model prototypes and glass domes, filled with mementoes. Jean-Christophe even custom-designed the Bauhaus-inspired pendant lights, in various shapes and sizes of paper. Sharp graphic imagery picked up on various assignments adorn the walls, and a collection of shiny block letters – propped up on the floor like an art installation – were salvaged from an old pharmacy. Sometimes a fresh look at things is worth its weight in gold.

Jean-Christophe's colourfully surreal vision extends to the glass domes, scattered about the apartment, which are filled with mementoes of past trips.

The majority of the flat's contents are vintage-shop or flea-market finds, including an Eileen Gray-designed ceramic screen (above, right) and a sofa by Arne Jacobsen (opposite), all of which contribute to the individual decorative scheme.

Street finds have also found their way into the mix, such as the block letters tumbled onto the floor. Jean-Christophe designed the Bauhaus-inspired pendant lamps, made from paper and ribbon, which are used throughout the apartment.

X

The kitchen bar in white marble tiles (left) was also designed by Jean-Christophe, while the cabinet, with its doors ajar, and Charlotte Perriand-designed stools were sourced from the Saint-Ouen flea markets.

A partition wall was added between the bedroom and the bathroom, a cool, dark space painted in teal. Such is the appeal of the designer's Palm Springs-retro look that the flat has been featured in numerous style magazines.

Yvan Mispelaere

A former circus-training base in a mews passageway has been revamped as a sleek and elegant modern space for a fashion designer

Upon visiting the Parisian second home of New York-based fashion designer Yvan Mispelaere, guests are left with the feeling that they have slipped into an intriguing, exuberant parallel universe. Inside the cavernous space, Yvan, originally from Normandy, has paid the same attention to proportion, colour and detail that he brings to the slinky, sexy shapes he creates for the runway shows and collections of international fashion legend Diane von Fürstenberg.

The apartment, rising above a gated mews passageway, was discovered as a rustic loft inside a former stable block, built in the late nineteenth century and later revived – briefly – as a circus-training base. It has now been reinvigorated in collaboration with Yvan's friend, architect Stéphane Ghestem (p. 108), who initially sourced the space, and whom Yvan, despite admitting to being 'very demanding', entrusted with the structural plan and detailing in his absence. For guidance, Yvan put together a book of tear sheets, featuring inspirations that ranged from the colours and textures of a sunken Moroccan sitting room to the architecture of Ancient Greece and the works of Le Corbusier. 'All of these are reflected some way in the scheme,' Yvan says.

'I wanted it to be chic and modern, with a more unconventional context and touches of the surreal.'

A cubic pod, faceted like diamond cushions in matte-black, contains the kitchen, and is set within an otherwise open-plan living area, bar the guest room and bathroom, which are partitioned off beyond the staircase. The angular design of the pod provides a striking contrast to the rest of the room, with its cloud-white colour scheme. Resting against it is an unusual bench, fashioned from a gargantuan tree root discovered in Bali. In the sunken living space, Ali Baba meets *Boogie Nights* in a high-glamour setting of sofas in burnished gold, by Italian design company Zanotta, and flowing fabric in shades of celadon and white. Anatomical sculptures, family heirlooms and jewel-coloured opaline vases, collected on travels, are meticulously arranged on podiums or under glass domes. Above, a striking pair of chandeliers from the 1970s, customized by Yvan with brass, evoke those that hang in the Blue Mosque, in Istanbul.

With plenty of room to entertain, Yvan likes to have friends and family over, and makes the most of the vintage Italian walnut dining table, extended with the addition of a white crown. Scattered about the apartment are brass objects that Yvan had made in Bali, including the ceiling lamps that shine down upon a trompe-l'œil cupboard, which opens up to a bar at one end of the dining area. Above are the master bedroom, a spacious dressing room and bathroom, the design of which is a nod to French artist Jean-Pierre Raynaud and features Yvan's self-designed winking tiles, underlining his sense of fun. Yvan designed the wooden floor to resemble mosaic,

and is also responsible for the bedcover in geometric leather. The matching wall lights above it were sourced from the L'Isle-sur-la-Sorgue antiques shops and flea markets in the South of France. 'I like a modern space,' Yvan says, 'but not necessarily the generic materials that go with it. I prefer finishes to be crafty, warm, textured.'

The thriving scene around the Canal Saint-Martin, an area Yvan loves for its 'authentic spirit', is only minutes away, yet his home is a nucleus of calm that acts as an antidote to his hectic schedule, not least, Yvan says, 'because it regenerates and inspires me'.

The kitchen is contained within a freestanding cubic pod, faceted to reflect the diamond-cut design that decorates a wooden door in the Louvre.

143

The flamboyance of the sitting area, encircled by flowing curtains and low-level Zanotta sofas, and punctuated with carefully arranged tableaux, creates a theatrical feel that continues throughout the open-plan space.

Dominating the living space is a giant sculptural cube, designed by Stéphane Ghestem, which houses the kitchen (left and below). At one end is the dining area, marked out by a vintage rosewood table and chairs by Frighetto.

The feeling of tranquillity extends to the grey and white-painted bedroom, tucked beneath the eaves (above and right). Both the geometric-patterned bedlinen and the wooden floor were designed by Yvan.

In the bathroom, the tiles, taps, cabinets and lighting give the space its utilitarian edge. Referencing the installations of artist Jean-Pierre Raynaud, Yvan has incorporated his own 'Peep Show' tiles, designed for Saint Honoré Wallcoverings.

Régis Dho

This artist and designer's white-hot space near the Place de la République has been injected with hits of bold colour, guided by the tenets of feng shui

Upon entering the home and workplace of Moroccan designer Régis Dho, it is the vibrant red colour painted on the wall that is the first thing one sees. Régis wanted to redesign his recently converted space along the principles of feng shui, and sought the advice of friend and expert Laurence Dujardin regarding the injections of dynamic colour, from the pillar-box red to the yellow highlighting in the kitchen and the soft, pea-green walls in the bedroom. Graphic and punchy, the colours pop against the brightness of the studio's glossy, white walls and columns and polished concrete floors. With the addition of comfortable, mostly white furnishings, and with very little in the way of the paraphernalia of daily life on display, Régis has created a look that verges on minimalism, but is by no means hard-edged.

Trading in a bucolic existence in the countryside, 50km east of Paris, Régis set about the daunting task of reinventing himself and his design consultancy business after getting the urge to 'get back to city life'. Wanting a fresh start meant getting rid of nearly everything he possessed. 'It is kind of thrilling to start over, and venture into something entirely new,' he says. Inside the apartment, his workbench is a long, white bar, designed by Régis himself to seamlessly integrate into the space, while also hiding away plenty of storage. On the worktop is a neat row of white porcelain cups, again designed by Régis (for French porcelain company Revol) and inspired by those crushable plastic cups, each is neatly filled with colour-coded pencils. His simple, bright designs and colourful micro-groupings, such as the clusters of yellow objects in the kitchen, energize the open-plan space. They also expose Régis's art-director acuity. Having studied art and set design at the prestigious École nationale supérieure des Arts Décoratifs, Régis has since built up a multidisciplinarian career with an impressive creative output that spans furniture, tableware, lighting, packaging and interior design for hotels and restaurants.

Having spent three months and going on over one hundred viewings in search of a place requiring renovation with the 'right potential', Régis finally found this 120m² ground-floor apartment, originally used as a military supplies outlet, on an unusually quiet, tree-lined street in the bohemian neighbourhood centred around the Place de la République and Rue Oberkampf. The entire flat was gutted and a massive skylight added to dramatically open up the space. It now flows freely from one end to the other, and there are no doors (except in the bathroom). Instead, there is clever use of partitioning, like the entryway where clients can meet around a Napoléon III-era pedestal table that Régis had discovered at a flea market and painted black. Here, and in the living area, hang bold artworks by Régis's artist partner Emmanuel Meyssonnier, along with designs of his own in the form of a limed-oak dining table and an elongated sofa (aptly named XXL), upholstered in ivory-coloured silk linen. A pair of canvas-covered bergères and chunky driftwood side tables add to the elegantly minimal look.

Around the corner from a list of bars and restaurants that line Rue Oberkampf, one of the capital's hippest nightlife spots, the apartment is a haven right in the heart of an area Régis loves for its 'lively and down-to-earth multicultural vibe'. But, he adds, 'In the studio, it is quiet and peaceful. It is a very special building to live and work in.'

This pared-back, coolly minimal studio space provides a calm environment for living and working, just moments away from the bustle of the Place de la République.

A dramatic entrance from street level is created through the confident use of bright colour on a partition wall, acting as a structural framework that delineates the space, and made all the more effective against an all-white background.

Work meetings are often held around the Napoléon III-era pedestal table (left). Above hangs an oil painting by Régis's partner, artist Emmanuel Meyssonnier; other works by Emmanuel are placed around the living area.

In the kitchen, a background of clinical white is heightened by hits of bright yellow and scarlet. Glass doors to the right of the cabinet open out onto an internal courtyard. The colourful groupings reflect Régis's background in set design.

The neat bunches of Caran d'Ache pencils are both practical and beautiful (left and above). The cups in which they sit were designed by Régis for Revol. He also designed the long workbench, which sits beneath the skylight.

At one end of the studio is the master bedroom, with its walls of soft, pea-green that warm and brighten the space, together with an adjoining bathroom. The restrained use of materials add to the look of elegant sophistication.

XI Victoria Wilmotte

The industrial cool of this rising star's studio in the Charonne neighbourhood has been given a modern update courtesy of her architect brother

The ceramic vessels designed by Victoria Wilmotte for her graduate show at London's Royal College of Art proved to be transformative. Catching the attention of Loïc Bigot, owner-curator of ToolsGalerie in the Marais, the smooth, matte-finish forms in tonal shades of blue and black were put into production in limited editions. Commissions from online company Made in Design and Le Galerie de Pierre Bergé et Associés in Brussels soon followed, including a bench, table, stools and other sculptural objects in marble and steel, all produced in Victoria's utilitarian style. Victoria has also recently exhibited at the Maison & Objet design trade show in Paris. At only twenty-seven years of age, her rise to fame in the product-design world has been meteoric, to say the least.

Upon returning from London with a degree in Design Products (under the tutelage of Ron Arad), Victoria spent a year searching before she found the ideal, light-filled space in which to set up her studio, vw Design. It is located down a small impasse in the Charonne district, the grittier side of the 11th. 'You don't find true industrial spaces like this in the middle of Paris anymore,' Victoria says of the ground-floor apartment, where the paper rolls for pianolas were once produced. As the daughter of architect Jean-Michel Wilmotte (whose recent projects include the Hotel Mandarin Oriental and Collège des Bernardins, both in Paris) and with three brothers in the same field, Victoria didn't need to look far for help in transforming the space.

'Victoria had clear ideas on how she wanted to make use of the space,' says youngest brother Nelson, who she entrusted to come up with a plan based around the need for a home that accommodated both living and work. Nelson devised a pod-like structure that fragments the space and creates a sense of intimacy. He used it to conceal the bedroom, which, with the tug of a curtain, opens onto the living area. Continuing the multifunctional theme, the bathroom can also be accessed from the studio – a hotbed of productivity.

Victoria's prototypes, made from solid oak and walnut, metal, marble and silicone, are visible everywhere – stools, trestles and side tables with angular 'walking' legs in bright pop colours, along with her ceramic vases, lined up along the shelves, are all from her 'Domestic Landscape' series. Other pieces include flea-market finds dating from the 1960s and '70s, such as the mismatched stools placed around the breakfast bar, and the quirky 'Workshop' chair, held together with fluoro-coloured wax, by German designer Jerszy Seymour. The sofa ('in desperate need of a new cover') is a prototype designed by Victoria's father in the 1980s; above is one of her own creations for Made in Design, a mirror that folds like origami. The whole ensemble is topped by a ceiling lamp by fellow product designer, Michel Charlot, for Eternit.

What inspires her own work, she says, are the everyday objects she comes across, sometimes even in the streets around her studio. 'I'm not looking to find a style of my own, I do whatever feels right at the time,' Victoria says – following in the footsteps of her design heroes Charlotte Perriand and Ettore Sottsass. 'Being able to live here in a "factory" environment is what motivates me the most. I love the fact that I can work on something all night if I want. I'm completely in my world.'

This converted workshop remains the industrial space Victoria intended, with the added comfort of a modern design by her brother Nelson Wilmotte.

The studio space is filled with Victoria's prototypes, made from varying materials in her distinctive functional style (right). The yellow pod that houses a washbasin (above) is an old prototype found in her father's garage.

The kitchen, an Ikea design, runs galley-style along one wall, opposite a breakfast bar lined with mismatched stools. The bar is topped with a double-sided set of open shelves: one side for kitchen utensils, and the other for books.

In the sitting area, the sofa is yet another prototype by Victoria's father, as is the blue metal chair beside Jerszy Seymour's funky wood and wax 'Workshop' chair. The mirror on the wall was designed by Victoria for Made in Design.

The bedroom is contained in a freestanding pod-like structure, which forms a divide between the zones for working and living. Hanging from the ceiling outside the pod is a pendant light by Michel Charlot for Eternit.

XII Philippe+ Patricia Jousse

A deft remodel and sharp contemporary design have given this penthouse refuge above the Port de l'Arsenal a pedigree edge

Conversations with gallerist Philippe Jousse on the subject of now wildy desirable mid-century modern furniture will inevitably lead to the works of France's most lauded twentieth-century designers: Jean Prouvé, Charlotte Perriand, Maria Pergay, among others. The designs of the era have long been a personal passion of Philippe and his wife Patricia, long before Modernist collectibles became the obsession they are today. The couple are founders of one of the world's most respected design galleries, tucked away within the vintage-trading triangle of the 6th, wedged between the Boulevard Saint-Germain and the Seine. Showcasing twentieth-century furniture and *objets décoratifs* both precious and rare, the gallery is a design mecca that also supports contemporary works by the likes of fashion-turned-furniture designer Rick Owens, and Dutch multidisciplinary company Atelier Van Lieshout.

The pair began to ply their trade in 1981 at a stall at the Paul-Bert market in Saint-Ouen, the world's largest antiques depot. 'At the time people were keen on collecting art, not furniture,' says Philippe. 'No one really knew anything about Prouvé and his work, not to mention that of his peers. So it became an education for us all, as we began to show people a way to look at this wonderful aesthetic.' Paris has its enclaves, but the area near to the Bastille, on the banks of the Port de l'Arsenal, where the Canal Saint-Martin joins the Seine, could be described as a 'no-man's land', according to Philippe. 'There's a certain rawness we like about the area, in addition to its lack of touristy features.' The pair stumbled across the two-bedroom penthouse apartment, which was being sold as a raw shell, when the 'typically boxy' block, built in the 1960s, was being redeveloped. 'The building itself was nothing special,' he says. 'But we knew that the views would be, and that we could really make something of it.'

Emmanuel Combarel and Dominique Marrec, who together form architectural firm ECDM, were given a relaxed brief from their clients, with the proviso that they incorporated such rare design finds as Prouve's 'porthole' panel in steel. Walls were softened with pigmented plaster, rather than paint, while underfoot, floors were poured with a cushioning layer of soft-grey resin instead of concrete, allowing the space to feel cool, rather than icy. A 'floating' stairway up to the rooftop terrace adds a sculptural element. Inside, rooms are peppered with eye-catching, covetable designs at every turn, including tables, chairs and bookcases by Prouvé, Perriand and Pierre Jeanneret. Artworks by Andy Warhol and Jean-Michel Basquiat are hung alongside contemporary designs by Ron Arad and the Bouroullec brothers. Also on display is the quirky 'Cactus', Guido Drocco and Franco Mello's humorous take on a coat stand, along with ceramics by Georges Jouve.

Philippe and Patricia wanted to introduce 'edginess, intensity and simplicity' to their home, and for it to have the 'easy-going, low-maintenance feel of a hotel suite.' Having achieved the look they were after, coupled with the views over the city towards the Eiffel Tower and beyond, the pair can indulge in their favourite pastime of trawling through the marché aux puces de Richard Lenoir, just a stone's throw along the canal.

Jean Prouvé's 'porthole' door panel, just one of many design classics that adorn the apartment, functions as a room-divider between the sitting room and the utilitarian kitchen.

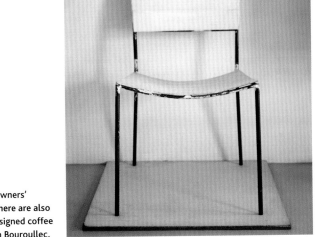

In this spare, elegant flat, the focus is on the owners' collection of mid-century modern furniture. There are also contemporary pieces, including a Ron Arad-designed coffee table, and a pendant light by Ronan and Erwan Bouroullec.

166

A large-scale image of the port de Salermo by photographer Andreas Gursky hangs above a pair of Jean Prouvé-designed 'Kangaroo' chairs from 1951. Around the corner, a *porte-manteau* in the form of a cactus can just be seen.

Philippe+Patricia Jousse

Basins by Atelier Van Lieshout and a painting by Bernard Frieze bring a splash of colour to the bathroom (left). In the bedroom (opposite), a Perriand-designed bookcase sits beneath Prouvé's 'Double Potence' ceiling light.

Stéphane Parmentier

An interior designer has introduced colour, light and elements of strong design to this former workshop in the 13th, just steps from his design studio

In the relatively uncharted 13th arrondissement, it is not uncommon that a well-worn façade should hide a contemporary haven. But finding such a compact, freestanding building anywhere in the city was 'always going to be a big surprise', says interior designer Stéphane Parmentier. The light, airy space, which originally started life as a key-manufacturing workshop, was redesigned by a previous owner in a purist vein, and offered Stéphane and his partner, artist Jérôme Tristant, 'the kind of flexibility we needed, and the bonus of a rare patch of open-air terra firma'.

Stéphane has long loved urban living, and established his design studio, which consists of a team of five, in what was previously a couscous restaurant, just steps away from his front door. 'Now I have a 20m commute and I love it,' he says. As an ex-fashion designer, once working with the likes of Alexander McQueen and Karl Lagerfeld, Stéphane

went on to develop his own women's line, all the while maintaining a keen interest in the architectural side of the design world. Making the transition a decade ago, Stéphane made a name for himself with lightning speed, receiving such plum commissions as designing the first- and business-class sections of Singapore Airlines and the latest Christofle flagship emporium in New York. His home is like a secret refuge away from the pressures of work, tucked away behind an early nineteenth-century apartment block, which has to be entered and exited before descending a long and narrow stairway, down past Jérôme's studio, to the front door. Leading past the master bedroom, a long hallway opens out to a welcoming, streamlined space. A platform perched high above is home to a reading nook, accessed by a striking spiral staircase designed by Roger Tallon. A marble-lined kitchen forms one end of the space, while a lounge area gives onto a small, central courtyard, with a lush wall of bamboo.

Wanting to keep it 'clean and bright' – meaning that there would be lots of white – Stéphane added warm elements, such as the dark wood floors, and designed a smart two-tone, melamine-topped kitchen table, a large, zone-defining rug, and smooth, rounded side tables made from hunks of lava rock (for Swiss firm Ormond Editions), which can used inside or outside. 'Balance and harmony are imperative' to his designs, he says, which follows his ethos of the 'need for purity', a bit like Modernist icon Mies van der Rohe – one of Stéphane's great inspirations. Exquisite vintage pieces are a tribute to other design heroes, such as a black marble guéridon designed

by Angelo Mangiarotti, and a walnut-top table by Warren Platner, a 'very special' first edition discovered at Paris's annual pop-up design forum, Les Puces du Design. These sit alongside more contemporary designs, including a low-slung sofa in plush black velvet and Tom Dixon's glitzy mirrorball floor lamp, together with Jérôme's sculptures and artworks by American photographer Alex Prager and German artist Peter Zimmermann.

Artworks and sculptures, including drawings by Mrzyk & Moriceau and a white Lasa marble piece by Venske & Spänle (bought at Art Basel Miami Beach), also feature in the bedroom, which opens onto a courtyard. With the sound of birds audible in the trees outside, 'we could be in the countryside,' Stéphane says. 'When I'm here I feel completely detached from the studio and what's going on out in the street. There is an incredible sense of calm.'

A mobile sculpture by Michael Cutler, dating from the 1970s, hangs from the ceiling of a book-lined niche overlooking this former key manufacturers' workshop.

The elegant main living space opens out onto a lush interior courtyard, and is punctuated by a Roger Tallon-designed stairway (right and opposite, top). Other designs, including the two-tone rug, are by Stéphane himself.

Stéphane also designed the round side tables made from lava rock (opposite, bottom). A patchwork of Parisian rooftops is viewed from the top of a stairway that leads down to the front door (left).

The pair of silver 'Nest' bowls on the kitchen table are designs for Christofle (opposite). Stéphane also designed the yellow lacquer and wenge tray that sits on the countertop. On the wall is a painting by Peter Zimmermann.

XIII

The master bedroom is a calming space that opens onto the adjacent courtyard (above). The bed is yet another design by Stéphane. A second courtyard is accessed via the bathroom (opposite, far left).

XVI XVII XX

These arrondissements form part of the city's outer ring, from the 14th, located at the southern edge, to the 20th, at Paris's extreme eastern point.

Today most of the Montparnasse district lies within the 14th arrondissement; in the sixteenth-century, however, it lay in the rural landscape beyond the confines of the city. It was unfortunately situated, surrounded by quarries that scarred the countryside – a dismal setting described by Victor Hugo in his epic novel, *Les Misérables* (1862). Sandwiched between the 13th to the east and its quieter residential counterpart, the 15th, to the west, the 14th has left the deprivation of the nineteenth century behind and today boasts the architectural jewel that is the Fondation Cartier, designed by Jean Nouvel and completed in 1994.

Parts of Montparnasse, which underwent a renaissance in the twentieth century and became known for its thriving art community, extend into the 15th, where its single skyscraper, the Tour Montparnasse, stands in lonely splendour in one of the busiest residential districts in the capital. On the city's western edge, the quartiers of Chaillot, Passy, Auteuil and the outer suburb of Neuilly-sur-Seine, all located in the 16th, form one of the wealthiest districts in all of France. Its elegant limestone mansions are among Paris's best examples of Art Nouveau architecture, as is Castel Béranger, designed by Hector Guimard, the designer of Paris's distinctive Métro entrances. Buildings by architectural designers Henri Sauvage and Robert Mallet-Stevens are tucked away off the wide and stately Avenues Foch and d'Iéna, and in the area known as Trocadéro, the Palais de Chaillot (built in 1937 for the World Exposition, replacing the Palais Trocadéro), has the best views of the Eiffel Tower and the emerald lawns of the Champ de Mars. Museums also feature heavily in the 16th, with the Maison La Roche (run by the Fondation Le Corbusier), Musée Galliera (formerly the Musée de la Mode), Maison de Balzac and Musée d'Art Moderne among the many.

Due north of the 16th is the 17th arrondissement, where two former industrial areas, Batignolles and Épinettes, are now mostly residential, with modest homes. The two other districts, Ternes and Monceau, possess the more glamorous Haussmannian housing stock. Perhaps the most diverse of all of Paris's arrondissements is the 20th. Positioned on the extreme eastern edge of the city, it is one of the areas that indirectly benefited from Baron Haussmann's push of the immigrant working-class residents out of the city centre during his modernization scheme in the late nineteenth century. Within this multicultural hub, the village-like quartiers of Gambetta and Belleville have been magnets for bohos and creative types, such as Hélène and Laurent Chapuis (p. 210), and furniture designers Ronan and Erwan Bouroullec.

XIV

Sophie Le Chat

In this Belle Époque townhouse in the 14th, an artist has created a comfortable home studio that retains the house's original elegant character

The home–atelier of artist Sophie Le Chat is, like her creations, calm and contemplative. It is, as she notes, an environment that encourages creativity, while at the same time possessing a modest simplicity that works for a busy family life with three children. The apartment is situated on the first floor, or *bel étage*, of a Belle Époque townhouse. This floor was once the landlord's level of choice, being not too close to the street, nor too far to climb – bearing in mind that there were no lifts at the time the house was built. Apartments on this floor generally boast higher, more ornate ceilings, larger windows and balconies, all of which are to be found in this elegant space.

At one end of the three-bedroom apartment is Sophie's atelier, where she draws, paints and embroiders at a large desk that sits in a pool of light. She repurposes all sorts of unusual, fragile and gracefully aged items, from antique toiles and soft kid-leather gloves, once worn to the elbow, to faded

maps, mostly unearthed at the nearby Porte de Vanves flea markets. Sophie is equally at home in the world of fashion, and over the past two decades has played an advisory role to the biggest names in the LVMH stable, including Givenchy, Louis Vuitton and Christian Lacroix, for whom she continues to advise on a marketing level.

For her home, defining a space that was 'simple and easy' was key, in spite of the classic exterior. 'I didn't want it to be overly filled with accessories,' she says. Instead, a few well-chosen, time-worn pieces of furniture – a vintage club chair covered in multicoloured striped fabric from Robert Le Héros, and a leather butterfly chair that Sophie stitched together herself – complement the artworks on the walls. Two oversized armoires also feature the worn

patina of age that she loves – one is made up in a patchwork of scrap wood by Dutch designer du jour Piet Hein Eek; the other showcases odds and ends – bits of crockery, framed displays of butterflies, hand-dyed balls of wool – that have caught her eye.

The feeling of lived-in comfort extends throughout the home. Floors are painted in a gentle grey colour to counter the crisp white of the walls, and ceramics by Dutch artist Hella Jongerius and Maria Hartikainen, a Swede, are grouped together on the mantelpiece. It is clear that Sophie has a penchant for the Jieldé floor lamps that are dotted about the place (at last count, she had eight, in a variety of colours), as well as for stringing together her own objets trouvés, such as the fishing-net floats the family found while beachcombing in Japan, and hanging them on the sitting-room wall.

'Japan is my inspiration,' Sophie says, and her admiration for the culture and spare, graceful aesthetic of the country shows. She is currently working on a cluster of Japanese paper vessels, with simple running stitches in cobalt and vermilion, to form part of a new series for a solo exhibition at La Color Factory gallery in the 13th. This knack of transforming objects into things of beauty in her work as an artist has been applied with the same sensibility to her home.

The apartment sits adjacent to an equally graceful building, with the ironwork grille of the balcony providing a decorative backdrop to Sophie's clean interior style.

A vintage children's drawing table stands in the corner of the studio (above). In the main living area, light pours into the spare, white room, with its club chair covered in fabric from Robert Le Héros (opposite, top).

The mirror-panelled armoire next to the small desk (above) holds mementoes and such objects as the Japanese paper vessels that Sophie uses in her artworks, and hand-dyed balls of wool, clustered together on the bottom shelf.

An old leather gym mat has been transformed into a rug at the foot of the bed (right); another was used to upholster the butterfly chair in the sitting room (see p. 183). From the ceiling hangs a delicate mobile made from toile.

The time-worn aesthetic of designer Piet Hein Eek's distinctive scrap-wood furniture is reflected in the kitchen cabinets (above and right). Above are 'Caravaggio' pendant lights by Danish designer Cecilie Manz.

XV Elisa+Michael Catoir

In Montparnasse, a husband-and-wife team have created a serenely elegant space for work and play, filled with their own quirky designs

Showing that anything can be the catalyst for a piece of great design, Elisa and Michael Catoir of Studio Catoir recently paid homage to style icon Audrey Hepburn by morphing a hat inspired by the film *Funny Face* (1957) into a bell-shaped pendant light with couture-like craftsmanship. The prototype for Ligne Roset now hangs from an ivory-coloured ribbon in the entrance hall of the couple's home, situated on an unprepossessing street not far from the Tour Montparnasse, the city's tallest skyscraper.

Many of the Catoirs' designs are scattered throughout the two-bedroom apartment they share with their daughter, Joséphine. Overseeing a team of twelve, based in their design offices in Paris and Milan, the couple undertake both private and commercial commissions; a recent project was for the Hotel Radisson, at London's Heathrow. Samples and mood boards are tacked up in their home office, which features a cardboard mock-up – for a design eventually made in Murano glass for a private client – which hangs above their desk. Elisa and Michael are incessant producers, and like to give these mock-ups a test drive against the background of crisp, white walls and chestnut-coloured floors of their flat.

In the sitting room, a large mirror in the form of a Union Jack – another of their designs – hangs above a sofa prototype, upholstered in deep-blue mohair velvet. The simple forms of the pair of lounge chairs by Elam, recovered in a silvery fabric, and Paola Navone-designed 'Log' side tables, alongside such cheeky props as a black-lacquered rabbit, work together to create an enviably uncluttered and harmonious space. Living, working and designing together, the Franco–German union began in Michael's hometown of Düsseldorf in 1997 on a student-exchange programme. But it wasn't until much later, after stints designing at Studios Architecture and for Andrée Putman, that the pair joined forces, working in Milan for eight years with Matteo Thun, one of the co-founders of the Memphis Group. Moving back to Paris in 2006, they established Studio Catoir.

Mixing traditional elements in fresh and novel ways, the duo opt to use local talent to carry out their designs, whether they are in Paris, Milan or Düsseldorf. 'The best thing is that we are completely free to experiment,' says Michael, and working across cultures in this way also offers the 'thrill of discovery'. In the dining room, there are stylish chairs, covered in iconic Missoni zig-zags and grouped around a Corian-topped table, which itself echoes the 1960s designs of furniture designer Warren Platner – one of their design heroes. There are playful ideas, too. In

the kitchen, graphic Vivienne Westwood wallpaper, a mounted stag's head and a pair of sheepskin-covered chairs by Charles and Ray Eames, flanking a classic marble-topped bistro table, together form a quirky dining nook. On the wall, a French platter has been turned into a light fitting, with a subtle glow creating a halo effect around its scalloped edges.

In the bedroom, bursts of vivid yellow complement the textural form of the rattan-lined bed. 'Tactility is so important in new design, because so much of it goes cold,' says Elisa. 'It is also important to be able to come home to a place where you can rejuvenate, that has comfort and lightness. That is what we tried to create.'

Humorous items, including this black-lacquered rabbit, bring some fun to the collection of furniture-design classics at this apartment-cum-studio in the 15th.

Neutral tones and natural wood finishes bring an ambient calm to the dining room (left and below). The table and 'Isa' chairs for Wooden Charme, upholstered in Missoni zig-zags, sit beneath a carved wooden bust of a stag's head.

In the sitting room, a pair of silver lounge chairs from Elam flank a Paola Navone-designed table, and provide a sunny spot for reading and lounging (below). The Union Jack mirror (right) is a Studio Catoir design.

Boldly patterned wallpaper from Vivienne Westwood forms the backdrop to an unusual dining nook, with its fur-covered chairs and porcelain-platter light fixture (right). Only the bistro table retains its more traditional appearance.

The couple's design prototypes appear throughout the apartment, including the 'Audrey' pendant lamp hanging in the entrance (left). In the bathroom, paintbrush handles dipped in gold form a school of fish, swimming up the wall.

To the left of the 'Oasi' bed, one of Studio Catoir's own designs, is a door that leads to the dressing room, where a paper screen by designer Mia Cullin can just be seen (above). The wooden chair is a vintage find from South Tyrol.

XVI Florence Baudoux

At this interior designer's home in Trocadéro, a makeover in monochrome provides an elegant counterpoint to classic French refinement

Interior designer Florence Baudoux cultivates up-to-the-minute Parisian chic, a perfect fit for the kind of interiors she delivers to her discerning clientele. She also consults for champagne heavyweights Krug and Laurent-Perrier, as well as designing furniture in collaboration with manufacturer Gilles Nouailhac, including the pair of Jules Leleu-inspired sofas, upholstered in candy-coloured velvet, which sit majestically in her own all-out glamorous home, painted in shades of perfect grey.

Although the space is typically French in its grand proportions, there is an abundance of light, quality materials and, above all, the intriguing combinations of light and dark that Florence keeps returning to. 'I had contemplated doing everything much darker – the walls, the floors,' she says. 'In fact, if it wasn't for my husband, the whole dining room would have been entirely in black – just like my wardrobe. But I toned it down a bit to keep everyone happy.' The luxuriously sized space (350m²), perched above a wide, tree-lined boulevard, comprises the first floor of a vast limestone mansion, originally built in the 1870s for the Comtesse de la Tour du Pin. It has been lovingly preserved and is now synonymous

with the *bon chic, bon genre* of Trocadéro. Soaring, 4.5m-high ceilings, Doric-style columns and gilt doors infuse the home with drama.

The apartment was the result of the search for a bigger space for Florence, her husband and two teenage children: 'I knew this was the one, despite its worn-out state, as soon as I stepped into it.' She followed her intuition, and revolutionized the space. 'Originally this was the party room,' she says. 'I love the fact that there was such a great social interaction going on here. But I really wanted to reconcile the formalities and open it out.' The great bones of the flat helped. After undergoing major renovations, the colossal sitting room, working area and dining room have been kept open and now flow through to each other, but the kitchen, bathrooms and bedrooms have been reconfigured to give the children separate, private zones. Florence designed a minimalist's haven in the kitchen, with sleek, black-lacquered fixtures, and wherever possible concealed electrics, heating and plumbing beneath the floors. 'The priority was to give the place a modern edge and enhance it wherever we could,' she says.

Florence then extended the mood with a monochromatic palette. Ever the perfectionist, she had six different shades of grey custom-mixed, according to the level of daylight in each room. Deep anthracite 'enhances the shadow' in the window-less entrance, and the subtle, calming pewter-grey on the walls lifts every splash of colour. A devotee of modern Scandinavian classics, including those by Hans J. Wegner and Poul Kjærholm, Florence also likes to mix things up, pairing Tom Dixon's edgy 'Daft

Punk' coffee table with a striking, one-of-kind dining table in white lacquer designed by Piet Hein Eek. Artworks and photographs are sourced from galleries with whom Florence has collaborated on numerous projects around the city, or are by artist friends such as the French illustrator Floc'h, whose works in bold primary colours, including one called *Samantha* on the mantelpiece in the sitting room, bring an individual edginess to the otherwise elegantly practical design scheme.

Florence's apartment in the 16th is a temple to Parisian chic. Propped up on the mantelpiece is an artwork entitled *Samantha* by her friend, the French illustrator Floc'h.

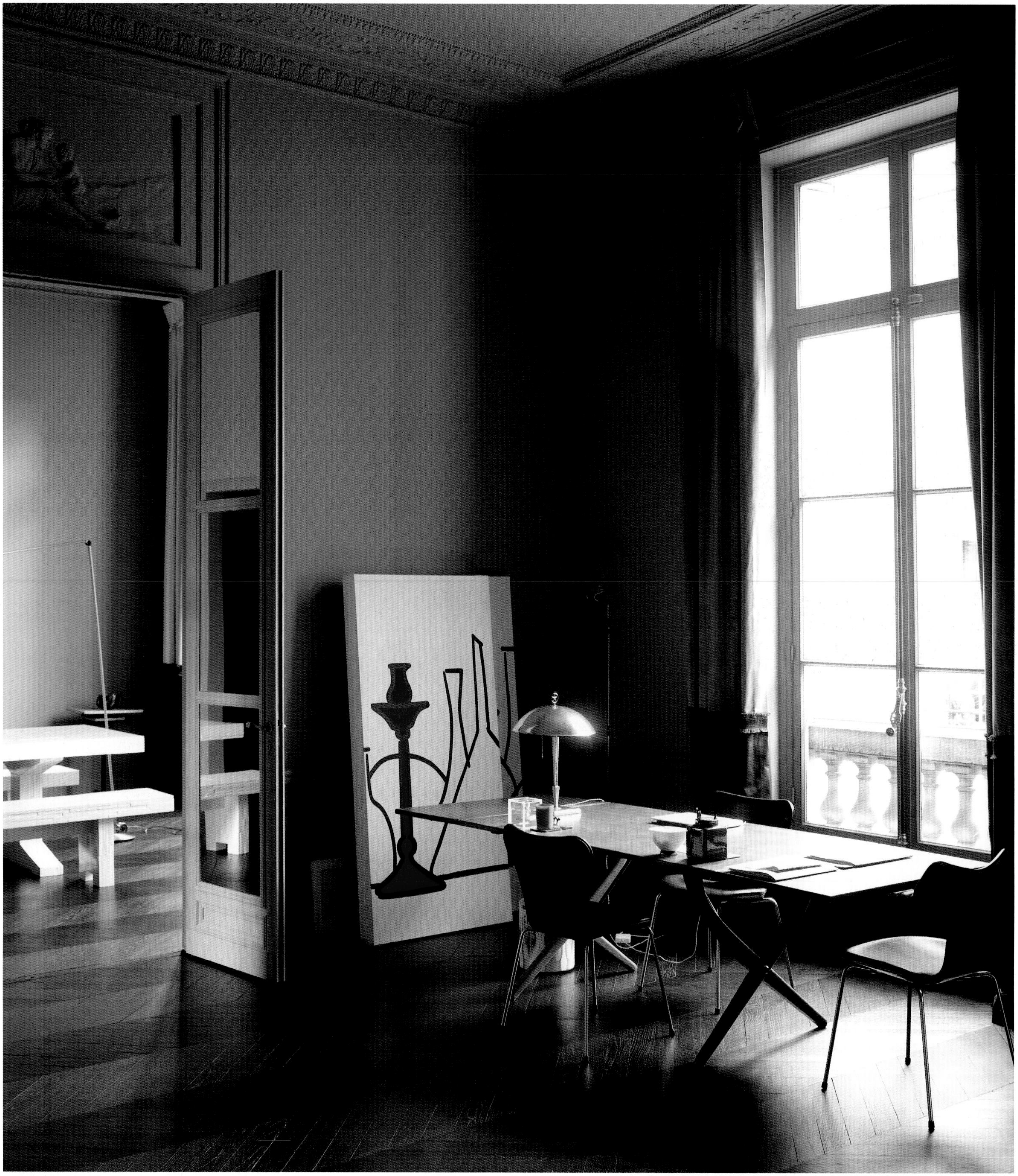

Throughout the apartment, strong contemporary designs sit alongside more traditional forms. In the dining room, Dutch designer Piet Hein Eek's 'Canteen' table is made up of white-lacquered scrap wood (right).

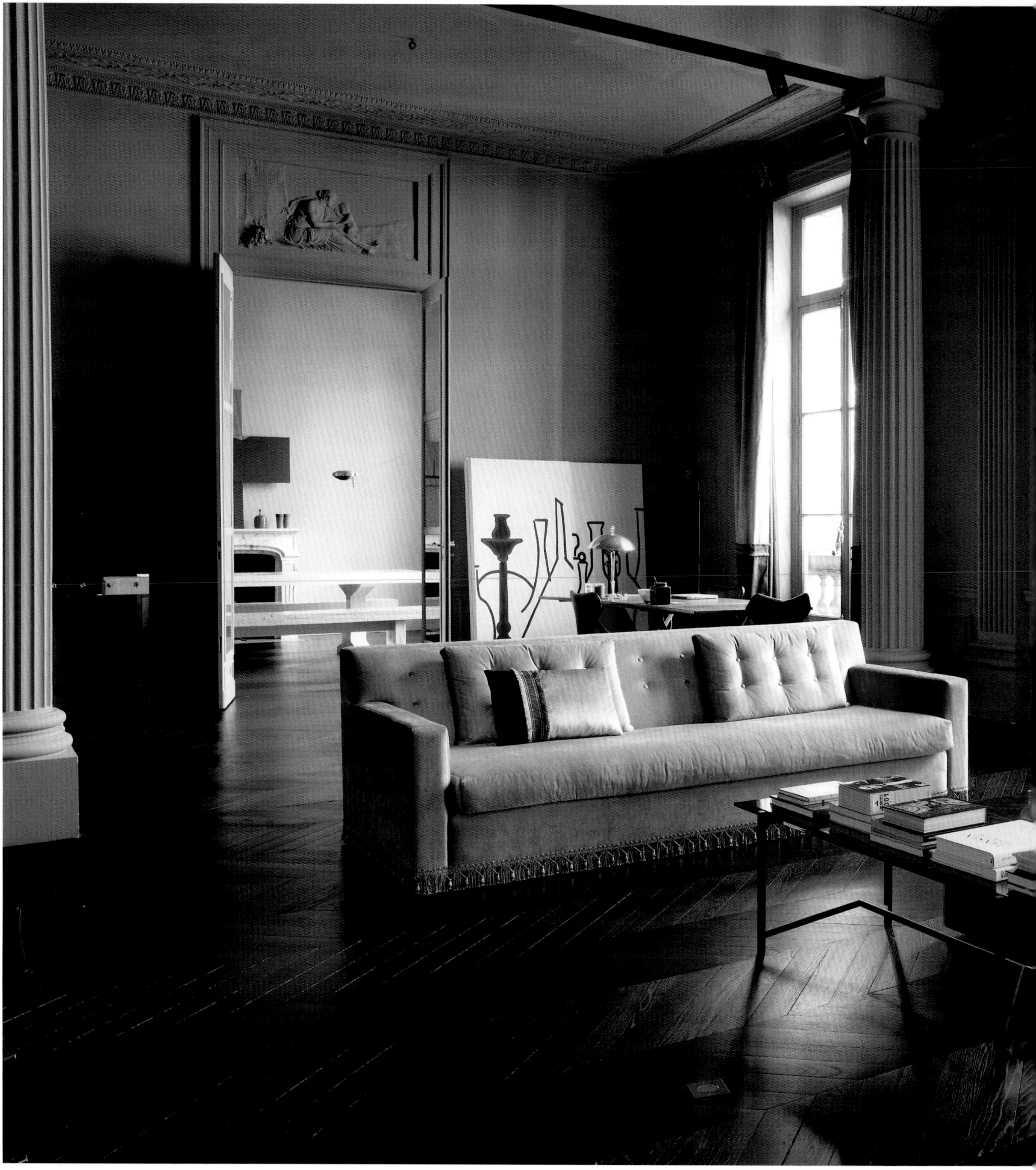

The velvet 'Saint-Germain' sofas were designed by Florence for Parisian furniture firm Gilles Nouailhac. On the coffee table is her collection of brightly coloured ceramics from the 1950s and '60s by Jacques and Dani Ruelland.

201

In one of the bedrooms, a wardrobe has been covered in 'Lorca' fabric by Osborne & Little (below), while the bathroom cupboards (below, left) have been lined with a 'Margot' design by Sandberg.

The shadowed hallway links the entrance to the master
bedroom, where a portrait of a cardinal by artist Christian
Courrèges hangs on the wall. A vintage vase by Royal
Copenhagen sits on a pedestal.

Martha Bedoya

This artist and jewelry designer combines cool pastels and vintage treasures to conjure up a beautiful *boîte de bijou*

All around Martha Bedoya's apartment, vintage objects and shapely pieces of furniture are unified by pastel shades – vanilla and palest pink – along with cooler, more glacial hues, against a background of Art Deco-meets-retro, with the Colombian-born artist's own handcrafted, sculpted or painted pieces adding a bold counterpoint. The overall effect is upbeat, with a hint of whimsy. If it weren't for a certain orderliness and rigour that underlies the whole look, one might expect Holly Golightly, draped in a cocktail frock, to sashay into the space.

As is evident from her apartment, Martha's personal style is uncompromisingly simple, set off by the unusual forms of her own creations. A pair of standout *tableaux des plumes* – large, circular black-feathered artworks – lend the space weight and gravitas. One, encircled in metal with crystals interwoven into its velvety centre, is a reference to the night sky, and has been with the artist ever since her design aesthetic was first honed at the L'École nationale supérieure d'art, in Nice. Martha has harnessed her passion for sculpting and working with gemstones into a dream job as an accessories designer, producing catwalk pieces for the haute-couture collections of Christian Dior, Valentino and Claude Montana, among others. 'I adore all that comes with working with precious materials, the exacting details in the tiniest minutiae,' she says. 'Seeing a piece through from its *naissance* on the drawing board to the end result brings a huge sense of gratification.' She has transferred a small slice of that glamorous world to her own luxurious and fantastical apartment.

Given her frenetic schedule, with frequent journeys between Italy and Switzerland to visit manufacturers, it is hardly surprising that Martha opted to keep her Paris home life simple. Her rented nineteenth-century apartment is located in a quiet residential street in the 17th arrondissement (she previously lived in the 10th), and was the answer to the need for a larger space. After several years of calling Paris home, Martha says she still gets a thrill from discovery, and takes inspiration from everywhere: 'I am inspired by everything around me. But then, just being a part of this city is all I need.' In the main living space, clusters of amorphous *objets*, a handful of which Martha has transformed into entirely new forms, are styled amid touches of gold, silver and turquoise. A pair of nineteenth-century opaline vases, atop a commode that Martha revamped herself with découpage, sit alongside treasures in the form of black-and-white Murano glass and porcelain lamps and antiques from the 1940s, basics from Ikea and flea-market discoveries, all of which have been subjected to Martha's inventiveness, whether altered, lowered, lacquered, or merely redressed with new handles.

The bedroom has a heavenly, other-worldly feel, thanks to its snow-white diaphanous curtains. Beside the bed, a delicately corded lamp sits on a white night table. The effect, like elsewhere in the flat, is one of ethereal calm.

Examples of Martha's own artwork provide a bold contrast to the background palette of pastel shades and cool, glacial hues in her spacious apartment in the 17th.

Martha's prized nineteenth-century opaline vases,
surrounded by shades of pastel pink, sit on a cabinet she
transformed herself with paper collage and lacquer (left).
An Art Deco starburst mirror hangs above the fireplace.

In the sitting room, vintage objects and flea-market treasures find a place in the soothing colour sheme. The feel of luxurious minimalism contrasts with the glamorous accessories Martha designs for haute-couture fashion labels.

Pieces of Murano glass recur throughout the apartment, and echo the cool decorative sheme. In the bedroom (right), sheer, flowing curtains in snow-white add to the serene, ethereal effect.

XX Hélène+Laurent Chapuis

This striking new addition to the Gambetta cityscape boasts strong, functional design and a luxurious connection to the outdoors

Fate and timing seem to play a large part in the creation and design of a truly good home. In the case of Hélène and Laurent Chapuis, serendipity also played a role, as the couple had been searching for a small site on which to build for over two years. 'We had just begun contemplating a move to the outskirts when this corner plot, an old car park-turned-storage warehouse, came up on the Internet, as if by fate,' says Laurent. Given the city's reputation for overpriced apartments, this gave the couple the rare opportunity to shape, from the ground up, what is now a striking contemporary home, stretching over four floors, in the centre of Paris.

The apartment is located in Gambetta, in the 20th arrondissement on the Right Bank, and has a village feel, with cafés spilling out onto the narrow sidewalks. Hélène, co-founder of multimedia agency Ultra Noir, and Laurent, a marketing director, describe the neighbourhood as 'downtown Paris', with turn-of-the-century industrial buildings mixed into the urban patchwork with more recent developments, making this area particularly fertile ground for architectural transformations. The couple handed the brief to Paris-based Argentinian architect Pablo Katz, requesting 'a family home with a strong, modern feel'. They wanted the house to be a blend of materials, including wood, glass, stone and steel, both inside and out. 'There had to be plenty of light and openness and a connection to the outdoors,' says Laurent.

Taking a year to plan, followed by another two and a half in the making, the result is a cube, lined in wood and glass and topped with a sail canopy over a rooftop garden. At street level, the stone exterior blends with the neighbouring millstone cottages. Inside, daylight flows throughout the house, with each level feeling private and protected, yet bright and open and loft-like. Floor-to-ceiling glazing, wood floors and bare concrete walls form a strong, textural backdrop. In keeping with the modern spirit, the pair picked out sculptural, mostly Italian, design pieces – a curvy chaise longue by Cappellini adds a shot of colour, while a supple white leather sofa and armchairs by Poltrona Frau are arranged around a bespoke fireplace, set within a panelled wall of steel. This steel wall acts as a divider between the sitting room and the kitchen–dining area, which opens out onto a terrace and a secluded outdoor niche.

Among the spaces on the second floor are a library and a reading nook, featuring a colourful 'Proust' chair by Alessandro Mendini, and up on the top floor is the bedroom of the couple's daughter Alix, and the open and airy master bedroom, with adjoining bathroom, with all-white and pale-oak surfaces that keep the space feeling calm and serene. Open to views of the surrounding rooftops and the adjacent park, the house emanates a warm glow, lit from within, when the sun goes down. Its arrival in the neighbourhood has provoked enough excitement, says Laurent, that passers-by will knock on the door, asking for a tour. 'That is the biggest compliment.'

The kitchen–dining area is separated from the living space by a panelled steel wall, which houses the fireplace on one side and the oven and storage on the other.

Up on the top floor, the clean, contemporary look of the master bedroom and bathroom is helped along by the use of an all-white palette and pale oak throughout, together with strong, spare furniture shapes.

A series of wooden screens with circular cut-outs lend warmth to the clean lines of the bathroom. Sunlight filters through the screens, casting a graphic pattern of shadows on the poured-concrete floor.

215

The house is a distinctive presence in this village-like corner of the 20th. Floor-to-ceiling glazing ensures that the building glows like a beacon at night, highlighting the collection of modern furniture designs within.

DIRECTORY (HOMEOWNERS)

Éric Allart [124]
Galerie Eric Allart
8, rue de Beaune, 75007 Paris
www.ericallart.fr

Jean-Christophe Aumas [134]
Voici-Voilà
31, rue des Petites Écuries, 75010 Paris
www.voicivoila.com

Florence Baudoux [196]
Luma
6, rue Madame, 75006 Paris
florence.baudoux@wanadoo.fr

Martha Bedoya [204]
marthalu24@yahoo.com

Elisa + Michael Catoir [188]
Studio Catoir
29, rue des Favorites, 75015 Paris
www.studiocatoir.com

Hélène Chapuis [210]
Ultra Noir
26, rue de Charonne, 75011 Paris
www.ultranoir.com

Corrado de Biase [56]
20, rue Béranger, 75003 Paris
www.corradodebiase.fr

Mathilde de l'Écotais [86]
2, rue Mabillon, 75006 Paris
www.mathildedelecotais.com

Jean-Philippe Delhomme [80]
www.jphdelhomme.com
www.unknownhipster.com

Sophie-Anne Delhomme [80]
www.sophieannedelhomme.com

Régis Dho [148]
Régis Design
90, rue de la Folie-Méricourt, 75011 Paris
www.regisdho.com

Vincent Frey [14]
Pierre Frey
47, rue des Petits-Champs, 75001 Paris
www.pierrefrey.com

Stéphane Ghestem [108]
Ekipment
36, rue de Lancry, 75010 Paris
www.abstrakt-architecture.com

Emmanuel Gintzburger [36]
Yves Saint Laurent
9, rue de Grenelle, 75007 Paris
32 & 38, rue du Faubourg Saint-Honoré, 75008 Paris
6, place Saint-Sulpice, 75006 Paris
www.ysl.com

Joséphine Gintzburger [36]
Joséphine Interior Design
30, rue Montmartre, 75001 Paris
www.josephineinteriordesign.com

Patrick Hernandez [92]
www.hernandez-architecte.fr

Philippe + Patricia Jousse [162]
Jousse Entreprise
18, rue de Seine, 75006 Paris
6, rue Saint-Claude, 75003 Paris
www.jousse-entreprise.com

Sarah Lavoine [24]
9, rue Saint-Roch, 75001 Paris
www.sarahlavoine.com

Sophie Le Chat [182]
www.sophielechat.fr

Florence Lopez [92]
Rue du Dragon, 75006 Paris
www.florencelopez.com

Thierry Marx [86]
www.thierrymarx.com

Valérie Mazerat [68]
vmazerat@mazerat.fr

Yvan Mispelaere [140]
Diane von Fürstenberg
81, rue des Saint Pères, 75006 Paris
14, rue d'Alger, 75001 Paris
29, rue François 1er, 75008 Paris
www.dvf.com

Ora-Ïto [50]
2, place du Colonel Fabien, 75019 Paris
www.ora-ito.com

Stéphane Parmentier [170]
62, rue Cantagrel, 75013 Paris
www.stephaneparmentier.com

Gilles Pernet [62]
42, rue Montcalm, 75018 Paris
www.gillespernet.com

Hervé Sauvage [44]
www.hervesauvage.com

Armel Soyer [62]
Galerie Armel Soyer
19-21, rue Chapon, 75003 Paris
www.armelsoyer.com

Isabelle Stanislas [30]
So-An Architecture
www.so-an.fr

Sacha Walckhoff [116]
Christian Lacroix
2-4, place Saint Sulpice, 75006 Paris
366, rue Saint-Honoré, 75001 Paris
73, rue du Faubourg Saint-Honoré, 75008 Paris
www.christian-lacroix.fr

Victoria Wilmotte [154]
VW Design
www.victoriawilmotte.fr

Pierre Yovanovitch [100]
16, rue de l'Arcade, 75008 Paris
www.pierreyovanovitch.com

DIRECTORY (SUPPLIERS)

ANTIQUES

Galerie Alexis Lahellec
14–16, rue de Jean-Jacques Rousseau, 75001 Paris
www.alexislahellec.com

Renoncourt Antiquités
1, rue Saints Pères, 75006 Paris

ARCHITECTS, EXPERTS

Céline Carbonell
celine@celine-carbonell.com
www.celine-carbonell.com

Marika Dru
Atelier MKD
2, rue de Chabanais, 75001 Paris
www.ateliermkd.com

Laurence Dujardin
www.laurencedujardin.com

ECDM Architectes
Emmanuel Combarel, Dominique Marrec
7, passage Turquetil, 75011 Paris
ecdm@ecdm.fr
www.ecdm.eu

Pablo Katz
11, rue Albert, 75013 Paris
contact@pablokatz-architecture.com
www.pablokatz-architecture.com

Angelo Mangiarotti
info@studiomangiarotti.it
www.studiomangiarotti.com

Nelson Wilmotte
Nelson Wilmotte Architects
13, rue Béarn, 75003 Paris
www.nelsonwilmotte.com

ARTISTS

Serge Anton
info@serge-anton.com
www.serge-anton.com

Nobuyoshi Araki
araki@arakinobuyoshi.com
www.arakinobuyoshi.com

Christian Courrèges
100, rue de la Folie Mericourt, 75011 Paris
info@christian-courreges.com
www.christian-courreges.com

Joakim Eneroth
joakim_eneroth@yahoo.com
www.joakimeneroth.com

Daniel Firman
contact@danielfirman.com
www.danielfirman.com

Clara Halter
www.wallforpeace.com

Nicolai Howalt
mail@nicolaihowalt.com
www.nicolaihowalt.com

Judith Huemer
info@judithhuemer.net
www.judithhuemer.net

Fabrice Hyber
in@hyber.tv
www.hyber.tv

Kolkoz
Represented by:
Galeries Perrotin
76, rue de Turenne, 75003 Paris
10, Impasse Saint Claude, 75003 Paris
www.perrotin.com

Edgar Martins
edgar.martins@edgarmartins.com
www.edgarmartins.com

Mrzyk & Moriceau
Petra Mrzyk, Jean-François Moriceau
Represented by:
Air de Paris

32, rue Louise Weiss, 75013 Paris
fan@airdeparis.com
www.airdeparis.com

Alex Prager
studio@alexprager.com
www.alexprager.com

Babeth Rambault
babeth.rambault@free.fr
babeth.rambault.free.fr

Willy Rizzo
12, rue de Verneuil, 75007 Paris
www.willyrizzo.com

Trine Søndergaard
www.trinesondergaard.com

Joseph Szabo
js@josephszabophotos.com
www.photosofteenagers.com

Vibeke Tandberg
www.vibeke-tandberg.inamarr.com

Xavier Veilhan
19, rue Fernand Léger, 75020 Paris
info@veilhan.net
www.veilhan.net

Venske & Spänle
vs@eingriff.com
www.eingriff.com

Li Wei
liweiart@qq.com
www.liweiart.com

Jiang Zhi
jiangzhistudio@gmail.com
www.jiangzhi.net

Peter Zimmermann
info@peterzimmermann.com
www.peterzimmermann.com

DIRECTORY (SUPPLIERS) – cont.

DESIGNERS

Ron Arad
info@ronarad.com
www.ronarad.co.uk

Atelier Van Lieshout
info@ateliervanlieshout.com
www.ateliervanlieshout.com

Maarten Baas
info@maartenbaas.com
www.maartenbaas.com

Ronan & Erwan Bouroullec
info@bouroullec.com
www.bouroullec.com

Mia Cullin
www.miacullin.com
mia@miacullin.com

Tom Dixon
www.tomdixon.net

Charles & Ray Eames
info@eamesoffice.com
www.eamesoffice.com

Piet Hein Eek
info@pietheineek.nl
www.pietheineek.nl

Pierre Gonalons
63, rue de Lancry, 75010 Paris
p.gonalons@ascete.com
www.ascete.com
www.pierregonalons.com

Konstantin Grcic
press@konstantin-grcic.com
www.konstantin-grcic.com

Maria Hartikainen
info@mariahartikainen.com
www.mariahartikainen.com

Richard Hutten
www.richardhutten.com

Hella Jongerius
info@jongeriuslab.com
www.jongeriuslab.com

Éric Jourdan
www.ericjourdan.fr

Hubert Le Gall
www.hubertlegall.fr

Cecilie Manz
info@ceciliemanz.com
www.ceciliemanz.com

Mathieu Matégot
psm@mathieu-mategot-furnitures.com
www.mathieu-mategot-furnitures.com

Julian Mayor
info@julianmayor.com
www.julianmayor.com

Paola Navone
paola.navone@paolanavone.it
www.paolanavone.it

Jerszy Seymour
www.jerszyseymour.com

Philippe Starck
www.starck.com
info@starcknetwork.com

Marco Zanuso
info@studiosoncino.it
www.marcozanuso.com

FURNITURE, FITTINGS, LIGHTING

Artelano
54, rue de Bourgogne, 75007 Paris

Arteluce
info@arteluce-srl.it
www.arteluce-srl.it

Cappellini
www.cappellini.it

Christian Liaigre
42, rue du Bac, 75007 Paris
61, rue de Varenne, 75007 Paris
sales@christian-liaigre.fr
www.christian-liaigre.fr

Edra
edra@edra.com
www.edra.com

Elam
info@elam.it
www.elam.it

Flos
www.flos.com

Frighetto
info@frighetto.it
www.frighetto.com

Gilles Nouailhac
87, avenue Niel, 75017 Paris
94, rue du Bac, 75007 Paris
contact@gillesnouailhac.com
www.gillesnouailhac.com

Jacques Charpentier
20–22, rue du Mail, 75002 Paris
thcharpentier63@yahoo.fr
www.jacquescharpentier.com

Jieldé
courrier@jielde.com
www.jielde.com

Julie Prisca
40, rue de Verneuil, 75007 Paris
ruedubac@julieprisca.com
www.julieprisca.com

Kara Mobilier
www.kara-mobilier.fr

Ligne Roset
5, avenue Matignon, 75008 Paris
paris.matignon@roset.fr
85, rue du Bac, 75007 Paris
paris.bac@roset.fr
99, avenue du Maine, 75014 Paris
paris.maine@roset.fr
147, rue Saint-Charles, 75015 Paris
paris.st-charles@roset.fr
www.ligneroset.fr

Ormond Editions
info@ormond-editions.com
www.ormond-editions.com

Pairpoint Glass
info@pairpoint.com
www.pairpoint.com

Poltrona Frau
www.poltronafrau.com

Rolf Benz
www.rolf-benz.com

Steiner
steiner-paris@cauval.com
www.steiner-paris.com

Wooden Charme
www.woodencharme.it

Valcucine
www.valcucine.com

INTERIORS, FABRIC, ACCESSORIES
Caravane
6, rue Pavée, 75004 Paris
caravane@caravane.fr
www.caravane.fr

Designers Guild
10, rue Saint Nicolas, 75012 Paris
frsales@designersguild.com
www.designersguild.com

Deuce
7, rue d'Aboukir, 75002 Paris
info@deuce.fr
www.deuce.fr

Goyard
233, rue Saint-Honoré, 75001 Paris
paris233@goyard.com
352, rue Saint-Honoré, 75001 Paris
paris352@goyard.com
www.goyard.fr

Jim Thompson
1–2, rue de Fürstenberg, 75006 Paris
www.jimthompsonfabrics.com

Kvadrat
www.kvadrat.dk

Lalique
Carrousel du Louvre
99, rue de Rivoli, 75001 Paris
shop.paris.carrousel@lalique.fr
www.lalique.com

Merci
111, boulevard Beaumarchais, 75003 Paris

Missoni
1, rue du Faubourg Saint-Honoré, 75008 Paris
boutique.paris@missoni.fr
www.missoni.com

Osborne & Little
7, rue de Furstemberg, 75006 Paris
france@osborneandlittle.com
www.osborneandlittle.com

Robert Le Héros
13, rue des Quatre-Vents, 75006 Paris
4vents@robertleheros.com
13, rue de Saintonge, 75003 Paris
lagalerie@robertleheros.com
www.robertleheros.com

Revol
www.revol-porcelaine.fr

Sandberg
26, rue de l'Abbé-Grégoire, 75006 Paris
www.sandbergab.se

Vivienne Westwood
13, rue du Mail, 75002 Paris
www.viviennewestwood.co.uk

MARKETS
Marché Paul-Bert et Serpette
96–110, rue des Rosiers, 93400 Saint-Ouen
Métro: Porte de Clignancourt
Saturday, 9am to 6pm; Sunday, 10am to 6pm;
Monday, 11am to 5pm

Marché Richard-Lenoir
Boulevard Richard-Lenoir, 75011 Paris
Métro: Bastille or Bréguet Sabin
Thursday and Sunday, 9am to 1pm

Puces de Vanves
Métro: Porte de Vanves
Saturday and Sunday, 7am to 1pm
(avenue Marc Sangnier)
Saturday and Sunday, 7am to 3–5pm
(avenue Georges Lafenestre), depending on tradesmen
www.pucesdevanves.typepad.com

Puces du Design
Bercy Village, place des Vins, 75012 Paris
Métro: Cour Saint Emilion
10am to 9pm
www.pucesdudesign.com

This book is dedicated to my mother, Helene.

We are immensely grateful to all the owners of the homes featured
on these pages, and would like to express our sincere thanks for their
generous help and support.

Particular thanks are also due to Ségolène Dangleterre, Véronique de
Goldschmidt, Ruth Hussey, Florence Lopez, and Christine and Thomas at
Gravemaker+Scott, together with Lucas Dietrich, Elain McAlpine, Sadie Butler,
Adélia Sabatini, Hélène Borraz-Bourmeau and the rest of the team at
Thames & Hudson.

First published in 2012 in hardcover in the United States of America by
Thames & Hudson Inc., 500 Fifth Avenue, New York, New York 10110

thamesandhudsonusa.com

Library of Congress Catalog Card Number 2012931637

ISBN 978-0-500-51630-0

Printed and bound in China by C & C Offset Printing Co Ltd